ON EXTEMPORARY PREACHING.

THE

DUTY AND THE DISCIPLINE

OF

EXTEMPORARY PREACHING.

BY

F. BARHAM ZINCKE,

VICAR OF WHERSTEAD, AND CHAPLAIN IN ORDINARY TO THE QUEEN.

THE FIRST AMERICAN FROM THE SECOND LONDON EDITION.

NEW YORK:
CHARLES SCRIBNER & CO.
1867.

PUBLISHED BY ARRANGEMENT WITH THE AUTHOR.

JAS. B. RODGERS,
ELECTROTYPER AND PRINTER,
PHILADELPHIA.

PRESS OF
THE NEW YORK PRINTING CO.

NOTE TO THE AMERICAN READER.

In publishing in the United States a second Edition of the present work, I ask permission for a few words of explanation. It is evident that the following pages were written for English readers; and especially for the members of the Church of England. I have not thought it advisable in bringing the work out in America, to make any alterations in this respect. I am not sufficiently acquainted with the methods and style of Preaching in the American Churches to enable me to make any attempt to address myself directly to those who minister in those Churches. I have only heard from competent judges that their general style of preaching is in advance of ours; and that this in a great measure arises from their having paid more attention to Extemporary Preaching than we have. Here therefore we have probably rather to learn of them than they of us.

My leaving, however, everything in this Edition

just as it is addressed to English Churchmen, will have for our American brethren the advantage of enabling them to understand to some extent which is the existing state of things, and of practice, and what are some of the ideas now at work in the Church of the Old Country.

I have always lived in the hope of some day being able to visit the Great Republic, that I might see, and judge for myself of the various aspects of Society in what is the last, and bids fair to be the greatest work of Time. Nor have I entirely laid aside the hope of being yet able to accomplish this long cherished wish. The more the two people see of each other, the better, I believe, it will be for each. May God speed equally on both sides of the Atlantic every effort to improve in any way Man's Estate.

The events of last summer added a fourth to the great, progressive, growing, imperial powers of the world. Of these four three are now Teutonic. In the face of these four great Powers the stationary and even retrograde Latin race ceases to be of any real weight in the affairs of the world. Their *role* is played out. The destinies of mankind have passed into other hands. And if it be in the Future that the sceptre of the world shall be held by the Western Continent, and that it shall become the centre of mental activity, and the home of moral and social progress, then the

Parent, his own day not having been ill-spent, may well rejoice to see his vigorous Child advancing still farther along the old familiar path; and as has ever been the custom of the race, teaching the nations how to live.

PREFACE TO THE FIRST EDITION.

On looking over my completed work I feel that it argument and recommendations are so presented as almost to assume the character of a chapter of Mental Autobiography. This has been done to a far greater extent than was contemplated in the forecast of the book. I find in fact that I have given but little heed to the proverbial caution, if I may be allowed a reference to it here, against admitting spectators behind the scenes; and which ought to be observed most carefully when the indiscretion to be guarded against is that of revealing what passes behind the scenes of a man's own mind. But I shall not regret having neglected it, if by so doing I shall have been enabled to impart to the treatment of my subject some of that kind of interest, which it could not have possessed, had it been dealt with in an abstract and impersonal form. Perhaps, also, it will be better that what I submit to the consideration of my brethren in the Sacred Ministry, should not be set forth didactically, but as the experience of a brother Minister of the Word. At all events, whatever may be the estimate put on my specific recommendations, most people will, I suppose, agree with me in thinking that it would be of advantage to the Church that some effort be made, and that is my aim, to improve the delivery of the spoken Word.

I take this opportunity to say that in the Notes and Studies of Sermons, which form the latter part of the volume, I had but one object in view—that of illustrating in some particulars my previous remarks on Preaching. In selecting the Sermons that seemed suitable for this purpose from those I preached during the time I was engaged in writing the first part of the book, I passed by all that were of a purely doctrinal character, because I shrank from dissecting, and from regarding, in a rhetorical light, the treatment of the most sacred of all subjects.

Many are asking how the efficiency of the Church may be so increased as to enable her to meet the peculiar and pressing difficulties of the times. No one would think of limiting the reply to any single measure, or recommendation. The following pages endeavor to direct attention to what I would beg permission to call a more instructed, and if so, then a more fruitful use of the oldest and most necessary of all the means that have been committed to the Church for enabling her to propagate the Faith.

Wherstead Vicarage,
Oct. 1, 1866.

PREFACE TO THE SECOND EDITION.

SEVERAL readers of the first edition of this work have asked what proportion of the Clergy I suppose capable of becoming Extemporary Preachers? This may mean, either what proportion of the existing body of the Clergy, many of whom, of course, are now incapacitated in one way or another for making the attempt; or it may mean what proportion of another generation who may be supposed to enter Holy Orders with the knowledge that they must, if possible, preach in this manner, and, therefore, who will all make the attempt to satisfy public opinion on the point. I have heard this question answered by another. Every Barrister acquires the power of speaking in public, and as the education of the two Professions is the same, why should not every clergyman? This is not a complete reply, because in respect of the point in question the two cases are not precisely similar. No one becomes a Barrister who supposes that he has any disqualification for speaking in public; while many who believe, with or without reason, that they labor under disqualifications of this kind enter Holy Orders.

Besides the subjects the Clergyman has to handle are much more difficult to speak upon than the matters of fact on which the Barrister founds his addresses. And the style, too, of speaking required of the Clergyman, demands more accuracy of expression, more smoothness, and more finish. Against this, however, we may set, for what it is worth, the consideration that the pulpit the Clergyman must enter every Sunday supplies to him, from the beginning of his career, more constant opportunities for practice than the bar does to young Barristers. And in large parishes, there are many occasions, and in all some, besides the regular Sunday Sermons, upon which addresses of one kind or another are now required from a Clergyman.

But I would ask any one of my reverend brethren, who may be disposed to take a lower estimate than I do of the capacity in this respect of the Clergy, to call over mentally the muster-roll of the Incumbents of the Deanery to which he belongs, considering, as he goes along, what kind of a Preacher each would probably have become had he through several years (and in this matter little can be done in a year or two) set himself resolutely to the task of acquiring the mastery of his general subject, and of the particular subject of each discourse, together with a proper understanding of the best way of presenting what he has to say to the minds of the congregation. Whoever will make this survey of his neighbors, will, I think, come to the conclusion that in the case of almost every individual, something far better than his present power of delivering the Word would have been attained. In some, of course, this point would be very far in advance of what it would be in others; and some would require a much shorter time to reach it than others; but, in every case, the gains would presumably be very great. No one would doubt that it would be so in writing. But as speaking is the most natural method of communicating thought and feeling, while writing is, if not an artificial method, at all events a less natural one, I believe that every one who has become, or who would have become, a moderately good writer, which is the alternative supposed, would with the same amount of pains, I cannot but think a less amount, have become a moderately good speaker. We must suppose a considerable amount of pains taken, because a Clergyman, with a view to properly qualifying himself for his sacred office of delivering the Word of God, cannot give himself less trouble than artists, barristers, literary men, or those who belong to any secular occupation do, to perfect themselves in the work of their professions or trades. If then this were begun early and resolutely persevered in, I believe the cases would be very few in which the Clergyman would fail in the power of grasping his subject with sufficient firmness, and of expressing with sufficient correctness and readiness what he had firmly grasped, for a discourse of half an hour. There is no question in these pages except of Clergymen who endeavor conscientiously to do their duty; it is, therefore, conceded that the writer of Sermons goes on year after year taking pains with the composition of his sermons, and doing this part of his work to the best of his ability. Imagine then, that instead of these pains having been bestowed on writing only, he had labored with equal honesty and perseverance at the other method of preparation and delivery; and whatever success would have attended him as a writer, would also, I presume, and generally to a higher degree, have attended him as a speaker.

I remember having been told by the present Bishop of British Columbia, (he was then incumbent of Great Yarmouth) that he had up to that time engaged twenty-seven curates—he kept what might be called a corps of six—and that in engaging each, he had stipulated for a certain amount of Extemporary Preaching. The rule was that the new comer was to commence with school-room expositions, and week-day lectures; and that after some months of this preliminary work he must preach without book once on the Sunday. Dr. Hills had found that in every case of this large number of curates, no matter what the man's antecedents, or disposition, or habits; no matter how timid, or studious, or unstudious, he might have been, the desired result had been attained. The man became capable of speaking in public. In this matter, I would not, however, apply the iron rule the incumbent of Great Yarmouth did, and with such complete success. Perhaps it would be better that public opinion should require of every Minister of the Word (a point towards which I think we are moving) that he should endeavor to the best of his ability, to attain to the most effective method of addressing a congregation on the things that belong unto their salvation. If, under such a state of things, one out of three should fail to attain his direct object, still he will have received no injury, either morally or intellectually, from having made the attempt; and the Church will be a very great gainer from the success of the other two.

One word more. We are obliged to presume that every youth who is admitted to Holy Orders, is already qualified for preaching the Word. At all events, it is our practice to exact it indiscriminately from all from the day of their ordination. This may be, and probably is, under the circumstances of the case, a necessity. It may also be really the wisest thing to do—to set the young Minister to work to learn this part of his duty in the best way for learning any thing, that is by doing it. A main part of the aim of the following pages is to convince the understanding and the conscience of those about to seek, or who have lately been admitted to Holy Orders, that, however earnest and devoted they may be, still they have many years of hard intellectual work in prospect, before they can hope to become thoroughly furnished and able Ministers of the Word.

CONTENTS.

CHAPTER II.

MY OWN METHOD OF ACQUIRING THE POWER OF PREACHING EX TEMPORE.

CHAPTER III.

SOME REMARKS ON THE COMPOSITION OF SERMONS.

CHAPTER IV.

SOME REMARKS ON THE AIMS AND SUBJECTS OF SERMONS.

CHAPTER V.

SOME REMARKS ON THE PLACE ASSIGNED TO PREACHING IN THE WORD OF GOD, AND IN OUR SERVICE.

NOTES FOR SIX SERMONS.

WITH OBSERVATIONS UPON EACH.

The object of giving these sermons, and of the observations that accompany them, is to illustrate what has been said in the previous part of the work upon the composition of sermons, and upon the way in which the modern preacher should treat his subject.

SERMON I.

SERMON II.

SERMON III.

SERMON IV.

SERMON V.

SERMON VI.

SIX SHORT STUDIES FOR SERMONS.

STUDY I.

STUDY II.

STUDY III.

STUDY IV.

STUDY V.

STUDY VI.

ON EXTEMPORARY PREACHING.

I do not propose to write in the following pages a treatise upon Preaching, for many treatises have already been written on this subject, without, I believe, proving of the use their writers contemplated. A failure of this kind might have been anticipated, from the fact that the writer of a treatise endeavors to take a complete view of his subject, and therefore devotes a large part of his work to what has little or no connection with the circumstances of the times and the wants of his readers. Both my object and my method of procedure will be different from those of the writer of a treatise. I shall limit myself to the aim of submitting to those among my clerical brethren who read their sermons, first some considerations in favor of Extemporary Preaching, and then a method by which in many instances the power of Extemporary Preaching may be attained even by those who may not make the at- 1. Object and plan of the work.

tempt to acquire it till middle life has been reached. In doing this I shall have to offer some suggestions on the composition and aims of sermons, and to touch upon some other matters connected with my subject.

2. Why confined to the writer's personal experience.

In carrying out my plan I shall only speak of those questions which I found myself called upon to solve, and of those difficulties with which I was myself confronted, in my efforts to carry out what I am about to recommend to others. Every body must feel repugnance to speak about himself, particularly on such a subject; and I trust that my readers, before we part company, will have come to understand why I am setting myself to do what I should have as much disinclination for as any of themselves, had I not what I consider a sufficient motive. I know that in what I shall have to say about myself there is nothing of any interest or importance to make it worth repeating for its own sake; and if I had not in view an object which I think it very desirable to promote, and which I think may be promoted in this way, I should not have a word to say about any thing I thought or attempted. People who are entering on any course will generally find something serviceable in the experience of those who have gone before; and what the events and thoughts of the day have brought one clergyman to feel, others may now be feeling more or less distinctly; and some, perhaps, may find that the course the writer of these pages adopted for carrying out his convictions may be pursued successfully by themselves. At all events, I trust that my way of treating the subject will save the reader from some useless discussions and unnecessary considerations.

3. Difficulties of sermon-writing at the beginning of my clerical life. My first year.

I was ordained in the year 1840 to the curacy of Andover, in Hampshire, a town containing a population of between four and five thousand souls, inclusive of two or three outlying hamlets, in one of which was a chapel of ease to the church in the town. But I confine myself to the subject of Preaching. Two sermons were required of me each Sunday. I began this part of my work, as I suppose was generally the case at that time, perfectly unprepared. I had not a single written sermon; nor had I ever attempted to write one, or in any way given the subject of sermon-writing a thought. I had supposed that, as I had some fondness for literary pursuits, I should find no difficulty in doing this part of my work. So I had thought. In the first week, however, I discovered that I was greatly mistaken. An historical or critical essay, of such calibre as might be expected from one of my years, or a copy of Latin verses, would have been an easier task for me than writing a sermon proved to be. At the time, I thought this was to be attributed to want of familiarity with my subject, and with the style of composition it required.

The experience, however, of twenty-five years has shown me that I was only partially right in this supposition. I now know that sermon-writing requires a greater variety of qualifications than perhaps any other kind of composition, and is therefore proportionately difficult. A sermon, just like all other literary work that is presented to the attention of the public, demands a certain amount of literary skill. This should never be wanting; and educated people have a right to complain when they find a clergyman undertaking the office of a public teacher and preacher without this indispensable requisite. But besides this it is necessary that he should possess a considerable amount of logical acumen, because every sermon may be regarded as the preacher's exposition of a portion of what has come to be a very complicated system of theology—of a system, at all events, which is controverted at every point. Another requirement is some acquaintance with what is understood by the term human nature, because the preacher has to deal with man's feelings and instincts, and with the secret springs of conduct, both with what is degrading and defiling, and with his purest and highest aspirations. A certain amount also of eloquence, or at least of the power of so speaking as to secure the attention, is requisite; for a sermon is an address to a present audience for the very purpose of moving and persuading them. I may also add, that if the preacher be unacquainted with the many very important questions arising out of the recent enlargements of our historical, critical, philological, and scientific knowledge, questions which are ever being discussed in society, he will adopt a tone in his preaching which will necessarily fail to conciliate the attention of the most thoughtful and best informed of his congregation. When I commenced sermon-writing, I was but scantily provided with any of these qualifications, and wholly unprovided with some of them; and, as I had to produce two sermons each week, it will not surprise any one that I found the task a very difficult one, and one which I was only able to perform in a very unsatisfactory manner.

4. The six following years.

I remained at Andover a year, and then removed to the joint curacies of two small contiguous parishes in the neighborhood of Ipswich. In the year I was at Andover I managed by very hard work, to write nearly one hundred sermons; but I was so ashamed of them, that on going to my new curacy I destroyed them, thinking that after a year's practice I must be able to write something less unworthy of my subject. I remained in this double curacy for six years, having on each Sunday to perform one service in each parish. As the two villages were very close to each other, a part of my morning and afternoon congregations was composed of the same persons. During the time I remained in these curacies I wrote three hundred sermons. I then became Incumbent of one of these two parishes, that of Wherstead.

5. Become persuaded that it would be better to preach *extempore*, than to read written sermons.

I had now been seven years in Holy Orders; all that time I had labored honestly at sermon-writing, and had thought much on the subject; but my thought, labor, and experience, had only brought me to the conclusion, that to hear written sermons read was unprofitable to the congregation, and that to read such sermons was very unsatisfactory to the Minister. In short, I had come to regard reading written sermons as labor almost entirely thrown away. Sunday after Sunday the same thoughts and feelings recurred to me. As I prepared for the service, while I was in the pulpit, and as, when the service was over, I returned from the church, there would come into my mind the thought, What wretched work these sermons are! I was sure the congregation took but little interest in them; and so that the benefit derived from them could only be indirect, and very small. I thought that they might perhaps keep up and possibly sometimes add a little to the knowledge of the hearer; but that this, if done, might be said to be done against his will, for I saw clearly enough that no one was intent on what was read. My thoughts and reflections on this subject invariably brought me to the same conclusion, that there was but one remedy for this unsatisfactory way of going on, and that was to preach to the people, and not to read to them.

I became so convinced of the unprofitableness 6.
of reading written sermons, that I ceased to write any more, and for the six following years the time I had hitherto given to sermon-writing I spent otherwise. This of course only made the sermons I continued to read still more unprofitable to the congregation, and still more irksome to myself, for we cannot take any interest in what we think slightingly of. My convictions, however, as to the remedy were growing into a practical form, or rather my convictions as to the certainty of the remedy were forcing me to devise some method for applying it. I put it in this way because I was well aware that I did not possess any of that readiness either of thought or of language which are necessary for extemporary speaking, and that my somewhat studious life had aggravated my natural deficiencies in these respects. I was what is called a nervous man; and having now reached my thirty-eighth year without ever having addressed to any audience half-a-dozen words except what was down in writing before me, the difficulties of carrying out what I saw to be right had appeared to me quite insuperable. Still I had gone on arguing with myself—"It is the right thing to do, and therefore it ought to be attempted at all hazards and in-

conveniences. No matter how disagreeable it may be, no matter what the amount of labor it may entail upon me, as it is the right thing to do, I must do it." I recall these difficulties that lay in my own path that any one of my brethren who may be supposing that insuperable difficulties are lying in his path, may be encouraged to think, that if he will honestly and perseveringly endeavor to overcome them, he will in the end succeed. I believe that very few will have greater difficulties to contend with than the writer of these pages had. If I had any advantage at all, it was that the practice I had had in writing would, to a great extent, save me from glaring inaccuracies of expression, and to some extent also from bad logic. But these are advantages which are not to be gained exclusively by the practice of writing; many who have written much, express themselves badly and are bad reasoners; and many who have never written any thing, express themselves correctly and reason well.

7. At the beginning, then, of the year 1854, after fourteen years' experience of the failure of the method of reading written discourses, I resolved that, cost what it might, I would give the remedy a fair trial, and that the trial should be this,—that for the next ten years I would not read a sermon; and that I would not do this in a partial manner from which little could be inferred, but that I would do it com-

pletely and thoroughly, for that during that time I would never once refer to any abstract or notes of any kind. I determined to read my text from the Bible itself (immediately afterwards closing the book, that I might not be tempted to make use of memoranda), and then to preach to the congregation from what I had upon the subject in the stores of my own mind. This would be giving the proposed remedy a real and effectual trial. It is now twelve years since I entered on this course. I have never in my own church deviated from it for a single service. The labor involved in carrying it out has been very considerable. It was so, particularly at first. But I never repented, nor do I now repent, of having made the attempt; and my congregation, I trust, are not dissatisfied with the result.

8. Reasons that weighed with me. Sermons often spoken disparagingly of. Not so with other kinds of public speaking.

I will presently state the method I adopted for carrying out my resolution; but I will first revert to some of the considerations which, while I was being brought to that resolution, were ever recurring to my mind, and which indeed I may say brought me to it. I recollect frequently saying to myself, Sermons, we hear on all sides, have very little effect; that portion of our current literature which deals with what is passing day by day amongst us, is ever speaking of sermons in a tone of disparagement, as dull and uninteresting beyond any thing else that we are expected to listen to; and this is only the echo of what we hear in society, and particularly in that portion of society which is most cultivated and intellectual. Yet every body knows how fond Englishmen are of listening to public speaking. Our public meetings, public dinners, addresses, lectures, and other things of the kind "in numbers, numberless," are very much the result merely of the desire to obtain an opportunity for hearing some one who is known to be able to speak in public. Even though, as a speaker, he may be below mediocrity, still the general feeling is, that it is better to have even bad speaking than none at all. The mind, just like the body, craves for food; and no kind of mental food appears to give such general satisfaction as that which is supplied by public speaking.

9. Fondness for hearing public speaking a characteristic of European civilization.

This is often regarded by ourselves as something peculiar to Englishmen, as a phenomenon of English life. But no such thing. If we go back to the earliest record of European civilization, we shall find that the Greeks before Troy were just as fond of listening to speeches as the Englishman of the present day. They could do nothing without public speaking. The chiefs never failed in this matter. They were, upon every occasion that admitted of it, ready to speak. Tacitus says the same of our German ancestors. So was it at the dawnings of European civilization, and so has it been throughout. Indeed, this is just one of the facts which distinguish the European from the Asiatic mind, and the European from the Asiatic civilization. There is a longing in our minds to hear the very words, spoken by himself, of the man who is supposed to be able to guide and to teach. We wish to see his mind working in our presence; to see his thoughts forming themselves before our eyes, and to hear them enunciated in the very words in which the thinker clothes them, vivified by the tones which no one but himself can impart to them. It would seem, in truth, that as there is nothing higher in this world than mind and heart,—indeed, as we are unable to form a conception of any thing higher, so there cannot be any thing more interesting to us than to witness this process.

Under our form of civilization,—and 10. Why so.
its difference from and superiority to the civilization of other races is the result of nothing but our moral and intellectual difference from and superiority to them,—the rule has ever been, that men should construct their opinions for themselves, their opinions being the guides of their actions and of their lives. No other system has ever obtained amongst us. It follows from this, that the mass of mankind, who cannot be great readers or profound thinkers, will always be desirous of hearing what public speakers

have to say. They will entertain the hope of being profited and instructed; at all events, they expect to derive from listening that kind of pleasure for which the mind has an insatiable appetite,—the pleasure which arises from having the faculties of memory, imagination, and judgment awakened and called into exercise in an easy and natural way, without any direct effort of our own.

11. The advantages the preacher possesses for public speaking.

Now it used to appear to me, that no one could be in a better position for ministering to this generally felt want than a Clergyman. No one has so wide, so interesting, so human a range of subjects to speak upon. Man's nature; man's relation to the unseen world; his duty here, his destiny hereafter; what will promote, and what will mar his happiness; what is the interpretation of the phenomena of human life—the subjects indeed are inexhaustible, for he has to instruct his hearers in that highest, that divine philosophy, which, if it be possible, embraces and harmonizes into an intelligible and well-compacted whole, every thing which man knows, and in which he is concerned. He has to speak to men about all that they feel, and want, and desire; all that they hope and fear; and all that they know. The man who speaks on political, or social, or historical, or scientific subjects only, deals with some one part of that wide field, the whole of which is spread out before the preacher if he be properly prepared for his work; for whatever bears on the formation of our feelings, or of our opinions, or can through these or other means be made influential on human conduct, belongs to the domain of the preacher.

12. Good preachers would be of much service to the Church.

How much influence, then, might the Church secure in this most legitimate of all ways (because it would be acquired by supplying the great moral wants of its people, that is, by doing its duty to them), if it had "a company of preachers" able to preach [1] intelligently and persuasively on these subjects! And I think that no one who is acquainted with the history of the past and the wants of the present day will suppose that the Church can recover the ground it has lost, so readily and effectually in any other way as in this. Other methods of proceeding may go some way towards reaching, or may assist in reaching, but cannot of themselves reach, the end in view. The Church, whatever else it may have to do, will also have to supply itself with this army of preachers able to handle properly their wide and sacred subject.

13. Shown by the history of the Church.

Consider the history of the Christian Church. It was in this way that it was established in the world. Paul and his fellow-Apostles came and spoke to men on those sub-

[1] Here, and throughout these pages I use the term "preaching," in contradistinction to reading written sermons.

jects upon which men were craving for light. Those were times when the old beliefs having become utterly discredited, and every nation of the civilized world having been thrown into the crucible of the Roman empire, to be disintegrated, melted down, and recast, there was, in a degree and a sense unknown before in the world, a mental "distress of nations, with perplexity." What Paul had to say was directly addressed to this state of things. It met "the present distress." He spoke to them of One who was capable of becoming to them "the Way, the Truth, and the Life." He spoke to them, and they listened gladly to the man who spoke to them on the subject on which they were so anxiously groping for light: and the work so commenced was half accomplished.

14. And so throughout the whole subsequent history of the Church. Whenever a revival or an advance has been effected, it has been effected by preaching, by speaking, by mind addressing mind through the medium of spoken words, on subjects about which men's minds were at the time greatly stirred. In none of these instances could the effect have been produced by reading written discourses. Imagine the preachers of the Crusades, or the Dominicans and Franciscans, who by their fervid preaching restored the then waning influence of the Papacy, reading written discourses. The incongruity of the idea is so great as to present a ludicrous image to the

mind. Their object was to move, to sway minds, to persuade. Who then, but can see that for them to have read what they wished to say, would have been futile and nugatory? It would have been to have thrown away their labor, and to have made themselves ridiculous. We cannot suppose that any thing else would have resulted from their adoption of the practice of reading. But to go on with this historical view of our subject. Could reading written discourses have brought about the Reformation? Or we may take a lesson from the practice of our opponents. The teachers of heresy have always been preachers, and not readers. Had they been readers, the Church would never at any time have had cause to fear their efforts. In that case their heresies could hardly have spread beyond their own minds. It is the eye, the tone, the living thought of the speaker, that moves and persuades the hearer. These will even give power to error for a time; and for a time, without their aid, truth itself is placed at a mighty disadvantage.

Had Wesley and Whitefield not been preach- 15.
ers, they would have effected nothing. I know they prepared their sermons beforehand in writing, just as Robertson in our own day did, and as so many other great preachers, as distinguished from mere talkers, did before them; and this is what I intend to recommend to my readers; and I trust that I shall be

able to persuade them that it is what always ought to be done to a greater or less extent by the preacher of the Word of God.

16. But I am understating the fact. Not only was the first establishment of our holy religion effected by the instrumentality of extemporary preaching, as were also its subsequent recoveries and revivals, and every stirring application of it to the circumstances of the times; but, furthermore, we find all Churches and communities of Christians so well aware of the superiority of spoken addresses to discourses that are read, that the practice has, I believe, been in all times and in all places to preach and not to read, with the single exception of the Church of England. The oldest Churches retain it, and the newest adopt it. With us alone the rule obtains, to read the written discourse. So singular a concordance, amounting almost to complete unanimity, under so great a variety of circumstances, does of itself go far towards demonstrating the propriety and wisdom of the practice.

17. The Minister of the Word cannot be, what he ought to be, a Teacher, unless he be able to speak in public.

But what I now wish to direct the attention of my readers to, is the consideration of the reasons which exist for our abandoning our present method. The Minister of the Word, as the title implies, is a Teacher—one who ministers, teaches the Word. But a teacher is one who is able to teach.

Sir William Hamilton makes the ability to teach, the one exclusive test of the possession of knowledge. It is plain, that reading a discourse on any subject is not teaching that subject. Teaching implies, first, the possession of knowledge, and then the power of conveying it, according to the circumstances and requirements of the moment, to other minds. A man who can do this, demonstrates that he knows his subject; and he is a teacher. The man who reads, does, strictly speaking, only demonstrate his ability to read what is before him. What he reads may be his own digested knowledge, or it may be an undigested composition, or it may be a mere copy of another man's work. But even in those cases where the minister reads what is strictly his own, he is only reading, not teaching. What a man reads, he wrote when he was alone in his study. The mere fact that, originally, it was written, and not spoken, implies a different structure of sentences, and a different sequence of thought. What is spoken is not always adapted for reading, and what is written is still more seldom adapted for speaking. The circumstances which give its character to the composition in each case, are widely different. In one case it is the expression of the thought of a solitary thinker, who is under no strong present impulse to consider any one but himself, or any thing but what is intelligible to his own mind. What is said in the other case is the result of a highly conscious feeling that other minds are at the moment in contact with your own mind. You feel that they are following you; you feel their wants at the moment in the matter before you. The congregation do in fact, in a large degree, shape your course, and give its color to your expression, and its tone to your language. You know that they are thinking with you; and this affects your thought and the form it outwardly assumes. This is one of the necessities of teaching. What is written in solitude can hardly ever be in harmony with the thoughts of the congregation. It is the transcript of, probably, the midnight thoughts of the writer. Some portions of it may possibly have been adapted from the works of others, some may have been extorted from a weary or unwilling brain; and when it is read there is little or no power of adjusting it to the requirements of the moment.

18. This his speciality; for good moral character is required of the laity as well as of the clergy.

I am prepared for the remark that the Minister of the Word is something more than a Preacher. I do not deny the assertion, but I deny what is implied by it. I reply,—Whatever else he may be, he is at all events, because he is a Minister of the Word, a Preacher; and when he enters the pulpit, it is then his exclusive and his high duty to minister the Word, to teach, to preach. To read, although what he reads may be his own composition, is but an inadequate and sorry way of performing this high duty. He will be wronging himself and his parishioners if he supposes that good moral character will be sufficient for securing their respect and regard; for of him is required furthermore that he should be able to do what he has professed most solemnly to devote his life to doing, that is, that he should be able to teach. And till he has demonstrated beyond all cavil and question his possession of this power, by the constant exercise of it in the pulpit in the face of the congregation (the only way in which he can demonstrate it), they can have no certainty on the subject. Good moral character, we must remember, is required of a layman, as well as of a Clergyman. The distinctive duty of the latter is teaching, ministering the Word in the most effective way he can to the flock committed to his charge. This duty occupies a primary place in the code of clerical morality, just in the sense in which courage does in the case of one who has undertaken the profession of arms. And that a Clergyman should never have given himself the trouble to acquire the power of speaking and teaching, so indispensable for the proper discharge of his sacred office, must affect the estimate which men form of his character. I ask my clerical brethren to regard this matter from the layman's point of view, and then decide what can fairly be required of them. In them this neglect is a moral delinquency. The congregation of the Minister of the Word who reads written sermons will perhaps treat him as if they had nothing to complain of. But congregations have hitherto shown themselves very good-natured and patient in respect of sermons, I do not think so much from indifference, as from a feeling of utter powerlessness to do any thing to amend what is amiss in the matter. But they may not always be so acquiescent. In their hearts they know that they have a right to complain; and already allow the mouth to proclaim what the heart tells them. Any Clergyman can judge from his own observation how much more respect is felt by his parishioners for one who, Sunday after Sunday, teaches the Word from the fulness of his own mind, than for one who reads to them, it is impossible for them to know, whose thoughts. It is in human nature to respect those who stand up before us with undoubted ability to teach us. There is no escaping from this feeling. If we cannot say of all men that they have more or less of an instinctive desire for knowledge and improvement, at all events, we cannot err in taking as much for granted of the members of a Christian congregation, because it is one of the motives which have brought them together to hear the Word. But whether this be so or not, it is impossible to refrain from respecting one who is manifestly our intellectual superior. Why, we even feel a kind of respect for one who is superior to us merely in physical qualities.

19. Its utility to the Clergy at vestry and other parochial and public meetings.

And it is not in the pulpit only that this power is indispensable for the proper discharge of the duties which devolve on a Clergyman. Without it, for instance, in how helpless a position will he frequently find himself when occupying the chair at vestry and other parochial meetings. He will, on these occasions, be distressed and disturbed by the uncomfortable feelings that will arise from his knowing both that he is appearing in a very unfavorable light before those whose natural, or at all events, whose official leader he is; and, worse than this, that the interests also of his parishioners, and so to some degree of the Church itself, are suffering through his inability to acquit himself in a manner which all have a right to expect of him. How often does it happen that a clerical chairman returns home from some parochial meeting with his temper ruffled in consequence of his inability to address a few remarks to his neighbors in an effective manner; and with a galling sense of inferiority to opponents who in other intellectual qualifications are not his superiors; and with a painful consciousness that he has been wanting to the duties of his office. And all this results from nothing but the practice of reading written sermons; nothing else is in fault, for in the majority of cases of this kind the Clergyman is the most highly-educated person present, and in many cases the only one.

But this advantage is neutralized by his having neglected to acquire the power of speaking in public, which it was his duty to have done, and for doing which he has more opportunities than other people.

20. Useful also as it enables them to give lectures.

Let me point out another very serviceable use which may be made of this power,—that of giving occasional lectures to one's parishioners. I know that matters of this kind will appear to some hardly worth mentioning; but any means by which a Clergyman can gain influence legitimately, ceases to be unimportant to him; and the influence to be gained and the good to be done in this way will be in proportion to the size of the parish. Such lectures will show to one's parishioners both that this Minister does not confine his labors on their behalf to what can strictly be required of him, and that his knowledge also extends beyond the limits that are usually set to theological studies. That theological studies should be thus limited is always to be regretted; but more so at the present day than perhaps at any previous epoch, because many departments of knowledge, bearing more or less directly on Biblical interpretation and theology, have of late years made great advances, some of them being almost new sciences; and the results of these recent advances in various parts of the field of knowledge have been very widely, I may say almost generally disseminated. Many minds, even in classes which a few years back had never been reached by such ideas, have thought of their connection with Theology and Biblical interpretation. These are facts, they are important facts, and we cannot afford to ignore them. The Clergy certainly ought to pay some attention to them. And if, more particularly in town parishes, the Minister should be able by occasional addresses to guide on some of these subjects the minds of his parishioners, the benefit he will do them will be great, and the sense of it will be so much added to the strength of his own position. And even in cases, as must frequently happen, where others may not be disposed to adopt his views, still their estimate of him will be raised by finding that he is not unacquainted with questions of so much interest and importance, and that he has formed his own opinions upon them, and is able in public to set those opinions before them.

21. Of more use to our Clergy than to the Priest of the Church of Rome or Dissenting Ministers.

The kind of knowledge I am speaking of here is required in an especial manner of the Clergy of the National Church. It is obvious that it is not required to the same extent of the Priests of the Church of Rome or of the Ministers of Dissenting congregations. The Priest of the Church of Rome is the minister of a system which ignores all the advances of knowledge. The old stock instances exhibit both the fact, and the reason why it is so. It appeared to the inquisitors who imprisoned Galileo that it was beside the question to argue from physical facts that the earth moved. In the same way the doctors of Salamanca treated the reasoning of Columbus to show that the earth was round. To their minds these questions were to be settled by theological, not by physical considerations. With the latter, the Priest of the Church of Rome has nothing to do. He is not concerned to know any thing of their bearings on theological questions. He and the faithful laity of his Church must walk without inquiry and undeviatingly along a path which has been prescribed for them by infallible but far from omniscient authority. And this in some degree accounts for the gulf which is ever becoming more and more impassable between the faith of the Church of Rome and the knowledge of its more intelligent members. On the other hand, the minister of the Dissenting congregation must, but for a different reason, act in much the same way. The bulk of his people, that is those for whose spiritual and intellectual wants he must mainly provide, belong to the lower classes and the lower stratum of the middle class. Of course many are ever emerging from these classes and carrying their Dissent with them to a higher and more educated sphere of Society; but at present the exceptions, I suppose, are seldom sufficient, except in large towns, to affect the Minister's duty in this respect. The bulk of his congregation being uneducated, or but slightly educated, can have scarcely any acquaintance with, or be but very slightly interested in, those accessions to our stock of knowledge which are the rewards of modern and, in many particulars, very recent investigations. In making these remarks, it must, I think, be sufficiently obvious that my only wish is to make it clear that the Clergy of the Church of England are in a position where it is required of them to come forward as leaders of thought. This arises from two facts: first, that our Church embraces within her pale far the larger portion of the highly-educated classes, that is, the classes that are acquainted with and take an interest in the questions I have been referring to—the questions that arise out of our recent acquisitions in the field of knowledge; and then, that she does not put herself at all in hostility to inquiry, criticism, and science. The Clergy, therefore, when they pay some attention to these subjects, are not to be considered as going out of their way, and giving up time to matters in which they are not concerned; nay, rather in so doing they are discharging duties they owe to themselves, to their parishioners, and even to that which is their special study. And they will be doing good by giving occasional lectures upon these subjects.

22. We should acquire this power out of consideration for the wishes of our parishioners.

In speaking of the conclusion it is the object of these pages to press upon others, I will not omit mention of a consideration which had some weight with myself at the time; it was, that my parishioners had

had no voice in making me their Minister; and that if any influential part in the selection had been allowed to them, in all probability I should not have been the person chosen; for I could not suppose that they would have preferred of their own free choice a Minister who was unable to minister to them the Word, as occasion required, from his own mind. It is just possible, I thought, that as they have been accustomed all their lives to hear sermons read, some of them may have given little or no thought to what is the best, or rather what is the right method of preaching. Or perhaps, the wrong method having been so long acccepted in the Church of England, there might have been a difficulty, whatever might have been the parishioners' opinion and wishes, in procuring for a small rural parish a minister who would be disposed and able, Sunday after Sunday, to preach extemporarily two carefully-prepared sermons. But these, I argued with myself, are only additional reasons for my doing what I am convinced is right in this matter. I ought to give my parishioners what I believe they would on sufficient grounds prefer. And even if, for the reasons just mentioned, they have not any clear and decided opinions on the subject as yet, still I ought not to take advantage of this: I ought to do just the contrary. I should endeavor to show them what is right and best. And, to take a wider view than that which one's own parish supplies, here is a practice which I believe is a cause of great and increasing weakness to the Church. It ought to be discontinued as soon as possible. The only way of bringing this about is for some one here and some one there, as conviction comes home to each, to endeavor to set the matter right in his own pulpit. Those who are convinced must begin with themselves. It is from those who begin in this way that the practice, if it be right, will spread to others. Already in every neighborhood one or two are to be found who have made a beginning. The effect of their preaching, although their sermons may not be in themselves all that they ought to be, proves that they are right. I will begin too. I will make the attempt honestly, and give the practice a fair trial. One's parishioners have a right to expect as much as this from their Minister. He ought also to undertake it for the Church's sake.

23. Not an answer, that the Church does not formally require this of the Clergy.

Of course there will be some who will deny that considerations of this kind possess any weight; because, they will say, the fact is, that in the Church of England the parishioners very rarely have any voice allowed them in the election of a Minister; and so we may legitimately infer that no attention need be paid to what they might have wished for in him under different circumstances. And again because, as they will go on to argue, it is wrong for a Minister to suppose that he can be wiser than the practice and than the authorities of his Church in any matter. If, then, the Church neither condemns written sermons, nor requires extemporary preaching, it is presumptuous in him to have opinions of his own on the subject, and still more so for him to act upon them. With these persons I cannot agree. A Clergyman ought to do what his parishioners ought to wish him to do, and ought to be what they ought to wish him to be. And though, as a general rule, it is proper that he should not consider himself wiser than the practice or than the authorities of his Church, still there are exceptions to all general rules, cases to which they do not apply, and just so it is with the question before us. True, the Church does not require us either to adopt extemporary preaching or to read written sermons, but leaves the choice to our own discretion, the practice of the universal Church, with the single exception of our branch of it, being in favor of the former of the two methods. To reply that one is unwilling to constitute oneself a judge in the matter because the existing practice is to read written sermons, and the existing authorities of the Church are satisfied with its being so, is, I think, to misapprehend the question. The very point to be considered is, Are there not reasons, both of a general kind, applicable to all times and places, and of a special kind arising out of the circumstances under which the Church's work has at this day to be done, which seem to make it very desirable that our practice in this matter should be changed? Doubtless it would be impossible to exact extemporary preaching from all existing Incumbents; by the time, however, that another generation had arisen in the Church, difficulties which now appear very great would have melted away, especially should public opinion become decidedly and openly favorable to the practice.

24. Why we must consider the wants and wishes of the lower classes.

We are too much disposed to think that nothing more can be said on any subject than what we hear said on it by our own set in society, or, at all events, than what is said by the educated classes. There may be questions which it is allowable for us to settle for ourselves in this way. This question, however, about Preaching is plainly not one of those that can be so settled. It is not an uncommon opinion among the educated classes, that it would be better if there were no sermons at all. It is also not an uncommon opinion among them that Extemporary Preaching is bad. They are fastidious; the faults, therefore, of bad Extemporary Preaching are distasteful to them. Besides which, it is often accompanied, as it ought always to be, by an earnestness of appeal which, again, is distasteful to many. These opinions are openly expressed and frequently heard. But those who hold them are not a very large proportion even of their own class, though their number appears to be very considerable from their being generally so well able to attract attention to what they say. Supposing, however, it was the whole of the educated classes that held these opinions, even that would be very far from settling the question, for they are not in the majority amongst us; and it was not from them, as is well known, that Christianity took its rise. The knowledge that regenerates and saves, spread not from the upper classes to the lower, but from the lower to the upper. Not the rich, not the noble, not the learned, not the powerful, but the poor, the weak, the despised of the world, were the first to understand and receive it; and it was from them that it ascended to the summits of society. They of Cæsar's household accepted the proffered light, three hundred years before it was accepted by the Cæsar himself. And if we were obliged at the present day to make our choice between the two in a country that had relapsed into unbelief, or in a heathen land yet to be brought to the knowledge of the Gospel, he who had considered what would most surely and most quickly conduce to the desired end, would prefer the conversion of the lower to that of the higher classes. The latter does not necessarily involve the former; but the former, if time be allowed, necessarily involves the latter. The constant pressure from the mass below on the few above, is far more telling than the pressure of the few above on the mass below. Besides, the upper few are ever dying out, and ever being replaced by those who emerge from the ranks below; and while those who sink from the upper to the lower class are worthless, those who rise from the lower to the upper are of the very best material. On this question we must not take the opinions of a rather talkative, but perhaps, in these matters, not the most influential portion of the upper class, for more than those opinions are worth; and if we find that the lower class, and a very large proportion of the lower strata of the middle class hold stiffly, opinions of an opposite kind, we must not pass by those opinions as if it mattered little how we regarded them.

Now the fact is, that these classes have very de- 25.
cided opinions on the subject of Preaching; opinions, too, the very reverse of those I have just referred to. They like Preaching. It is their chief intellectual pleasure and excitement. There is not any great variety of conversation in the society they frequent. They are not much given to reading novels or daily papers; nor do they attend theatres. Sermons occupy a much larger space in their thoughts than they do in the thoughts of those whose minds are fed with a great variety of other food. Religion, too, with them is a more serious and engrossing matter. They are more conversant with the cares than with the pleasures of the world. Either by a simple process of reasoning, such as we might expect in them, or because they have taken up the idea from their Dis-

senting neighbors (but perhaps their opinions on this subject rest on both these foundations), they have come to think that he is only a pretended Minister of the Word, who cannot in his own pulpit minister the Word from the stores of his own mind. He who, when he mislays or forgets his manuscript, is obliged to close the service without a sermon, they will not regard as a Minister of the Word. They hear our opponents calling such Ministers "hirelings" and "dumb dogs," and some of them have come to repeat the opprobrious terms. It will never do for us to neglect (there are good reasons for our carefully considering) the opinions of these classes. Their opinions, by a constant pressure from below, and by the rise of many from these classes to those above, are spreading upward. And is it fair to a large part of our congregations that we should put them in the disagreeable position of hearing their Minister taunted in this way by our opponents? And if they are unable to answer these taunts, does not that give rise to a probability that they will not always be able to bear them?

26. Hitherto I have been recalling thoughts which frequently occupied my mind before I commenced the practice of Extemporary Preaching, and which at last determined me to make the attempt. I will now proceed to some questions which the adoption of the practice will at times oblige one to discuss or con-

sider. I shall then describe the method I pursued for carrying out my determination, and afterwards give so much of the results of my experience in the composition of sermons, and on some other kindred subjects, as I suppose may be of some use to others.

27. How the question—Which is best, to read written sermons, or to preach *extempore?* ought to be put.

One way, but a wholly inadequate way, of putting the question raised in these pages, is to ask at once, Which would be the best, a sermon written and read, or one on the same subject preached extemporarily, by the same person? I am prepared to hear many, both among the laity and the clergy, exclaim unhesitatingly, "The one that is written and read, because, at all events, it will be more carefully composed." In the course of what I have yet to say, I trust that I shall be able to bring my readers to see that the very reverse of this ought to be, and will generally be the case; but what I now wish to show is, how this question ought to be put. The comparison must be made, not between the written and the extemporary sermons of a man who has had some practice in writing and none in Extemporary Preaching, but of one who has given himself the trouble to put his power of Extemporary Preaching somewhat on a level with his attainments in written composition; for of course there can be no comparison between the sermons of one who has not done this. Such an one may have acquired the power of writing with, as the case may be, more or less skill, but may not have acquired any power at all of Extemporary Preaching. In his case, therefore, the comparison would be between something and nothing. Another point to be settled in the consideration of this question is, What is meant by the best sermon? Plainly not the one that will read the best when in print, for primarily, and *ex vi termini*, a sermon is something intended to be spoken and heard, not something to be read; and what we are speaking about is not reading, but hearing sermons. The merits, then, of sermons are to be decided by the effect they respectively produce upon a present listening congregation. The question before us, therefore, is this: Which will produce the most powerful, abiding, and beneficial effect, a written and read sermon, or an extemporary sermon; both being delivered by a man who has paid as much attention to the one method as to the other; or, if they are preached by different persons, they must be persons of equal ability and attainments, and who have had equal practice in their respective styles of composition and delivery? If the question be put in this way, and it is the only fair way of putting it, I can hardly imagine any clergyman who has made some proficiency in the practice of speaking, or any congregation that listens to such a speaker, hesitating a moment for a reply to the question. This is one of those questions which to state properly is to answer. I need not, however, in this place, say any thing more directly upon it, because a great part of the contents of these pages are a reply to it; every thing indeed throughout them having reference to it. Here I only wish to show how the question ought to be put.

28. Extemporary Preaching secures continuous study and improvement.

I proceed to another point; we should most of us be benefited by any method of carrying on our work which might, as a general rule secure continuous improvement in the composition and delivery of our sermons. My own experience has taught me that writing and reading one's sermons does not effect this, but that preaching extemporarily sermons as carefully studied as extemporary sermons always ought to be, does effect it. Bacon tells us that reading makes a full man, writing an accurate man, and speaking a ready man. What I recommend embraces these three kinds of discipline. The Extemporary Preacher who is in the constant practice of properly studying his subject with the view of making his discourse as worthy of his office and as effective as possible, will be drawn on into many fields of inquiry. So also it may be said will the writer of sermons; but not, I think so continuously, or with so much benefit to himself. The man who preaches extemporarily, that is, who gives himself the trouble to do it properly, must have the subject-matter of his sermons very frequently in his thoughts, and must give himself a great deal of trouble in perfecting every sermon he preaches; and this amount of thought directed to his work will bring him sooner or later to understand what materials his sermons require. He will thus be led on to be ever adding to his critical, historical, and philological knowledge; he will keep up and extend his acquaintance with the works of the great writers on ethical science; nor will he allow himself to be ignorant of the controversies of the present or of past times. He will find these kinds of knowledge necessary, because he will find that there are parts of his subject which it will be impossible for him to handle properly without them. He will, I think, become a far deeper and more varied student than the man who reads written sermons. He is likely to read more, and certainly to digest more completely the fruits of his reading, and to make them more completely his own. The man who reads written sermons, supposing him to have started with an equally conscientious desire to do his work thoroughly, is not under the same pressure and impulsion to study widely and deeply, and to make the fruits of his study his own. The pressure is neither so strong nor so continuous. His method does not require it. He has to produce something on paper, and not in his own mind. There is a wide difference between these two ways of working, and these two kinds of work. He has not so constantly before his mind that which is the end of speaking—the effect to be produced. When the writer of sermons has seven or eight hundred by him, he must be very different from the generality of mankind if he still continues the labor of writing week after week. And indeed, why should he? He has nothing fresh to write upon; and after so much practice in writing, he can hardly hope to produce any thing better than what he has ready at hand. With the Extemporary Preacher it is quite another thing. His work is never done. His weekly preparation is incessant. His studies can never be laid aside. Still as he grows old he learns something every day. Of course, I never speak of the ignorant ranter, the frothy declaimer, or the fluent talker. Their way of discoursing will always astonish the multitude, but that is not what will satisfy the man who has a proper respect for himself, for his congregation, and for his sacred office. He will study more or less for every sermon, and will make out, after careful consideration, the form in which his materials should be arranged on every occasion: every occasion thus becoming a fresh study both for matter and form. There can therefore be no doubt but that in a course of years he will acquire more, and learn better how to use what he has acquired, than a reader of written sermons.

29. As it presupposes writing, it will also secure accuracy.

Nor will the practice of Extemporary Preaching deprive a man of the advantage of attaining to that accuracy which is a result of written composition. I am addressing myself to those who have energy enough to persevere for some years, or for whatever time may be required, in the practice of carefully composing their sermons during the week, and then preaching them extemporarily on the Sunday. The time will come when full notes, containing only the more important parts *in extenso*, will be sufficient; and at last nothing more will in most cases be needed than such a sketch as may be written on one side of half a sheet of note-paper, the rest of the study being carried on mentally, or without the aid of writing. I suppose that for several years more or less of writing will be necessary, because that alone will demonstrate to the preacher that he has mastered his subject and properly arranged his materials; and so will enable his mind to rest on the fact that it has already produced what it now has only to reproduce in the pulpit. And I can imagine persons preferring to the last to write very full abstracts of what they intend to say, and doing this from a religious regard for their work. A sermon, such persons will feel, is too important a work, too much depends upon it, to justify the preacher in leaving any thing to the chances of the moment. This must be done to some extent in a debate, and it may be done generally in secular oratory, when the main object is to please; but it is irreverent and unwise to trust in this way to the moment for the matter or the arrangement of a sermon: it will, therefore, I think, be better that the preacher, however practised, should never wholly lay aside the pen. He might perhaps do without it, and the majority of his congregation be none the less pleased with him; but there will always be some who would have more highly appreciated a better studied and more carefully arranged address. The preacher, too, ought to be much dissatisfied with himself should he fail to give his subject every advantage. He will be aware whether it could have been put better; and if so, the knowledge of how his subject and congregation have suffered by his negligence ought to distress him. We find that the most perfect masters of ancient oratory wrote their speeches: there are additional reasons for the preachers of the Word doing the same. I think then that we may conclude that, as a class, the Extemporary Preachers will be fuller, not less accurate, and certainly readier men than the readers of written sermons.

30. This is the natural and most impressive method of delivery.

Another very important advantage possessed by the Extemporary Preacher is the superiority of his method of delivery. One of the first objects of the preacher and of the reader alike must be to gain the attention of the audience. In his efforts to do this, the preacher follows the natural method—the method every one is using all his life through, and with the application of which to himself every one is equally familiar. It is the method of conversation. It is the only way in which men use language in their face-to-face intercourse with each other. When a man speaks to another, the auditor feels that his attention is challenged, and therefore attention is given as a matter of course and of habit. It would be unreasonable if the auditor did not attend. The speaker is speaking to him. There seems no room for choice. The auditor is called upon not only to attend, but to do what attention to a speaker implies, to remember, and to judge of what is being said. This is understood by what is seen of the present working of the mind of the speaker, in the play of his features, in the tones of his voice, and in the direct bearing of what he is saying, either by way of explanation, illustration, or appeal, on the actual feelings of the hearers, or on the thoughts that are at that moment in their minds. Contrast with this the effect of reading. I hardly need go into particulars. This is not the natural mode of address. It is a mode with which no one can be familiar. It does not challenge attention. We feel that the reader's mind is not directed to our mind, as a speaker's would be; but rather that it is addressed to an imaginary mind. It is addressed to an imaginary unbeliever, or an imaginary misbeliever, to an imaginary worldling, or to an imaginary wrong-doer of some kind or other. It is not addressed to what is passing in the minds of the men and women then and there present. And, as a matter of fact, the effect corresponds with this difference; and the reader fails to gain attention to that degree which is accorded without any effort on the part of the congregation to the Extemporary Preacher. We all know that reading does not possess the requisites for enabling it always to command our attention. And after all there are reasonable grounds why the congregation should not make much effort to listen to what is read. It is not the living mind that is wrestling with their minds, but in reality a MS., which through the medium of the reader's voice, is addressing them. It is the MS. that is dealing with them, a MS. which they might read for themselves with as much profit perhaps as they will derive from hearing it read to them.

31. Answer to the objection that it is an offering which costs nothing.

I will now advert to two most opposite objections on this subject, both of which are frequently urged; both, however, of which result from a misapprehension of what is meant by Extemporary Preaching. I have heard a clergyman say that he disliked the practice, "because, like David, he would not make an offering unto the Lord his God of that which cost him nothing." My reply to him was, that I thought that his objection might more frequently be levelled at sermons that are read than at those that are preached extemporarily. The most conscientious reader of written sermons most frequently read what on the occasion of his reading it, cost him nothing, inasmuch as it was written years before. This, however, can never be the case with the conscientious Extemporary Preacher, for, as every sermon he preaches must be studied, his preaching is indeed a perpetual offering of that which costs him much. To be prepared every Sunday of his life, however busy he may have been during the week about other matters, with two carefully studied sermons, though not more than the Minister of the Word ought to do, is more, I am disposed to think, than those who are capable of quoting David's sentiment as a reason for rejecting Extemporary Preaching, are ever likely to do themselves. This objection may be valid against those who enter the pulpit merely to declaim, or to talk incoherently on religious subjects for half an hour—it is not uncharitable to say,—in accordance rather with the darkness than with any light that is within them. But I would put in the balance against such preachers a class which must be far more numerous—that of the readers of unimpressive, uninteresting, and unprofitable sermons, and who, as long as they continue to be readers, will never improve; and here we must not forget that the laity tell us that to listen to such sermons is on their part an offering which costs them much.

32. And that it takes too much time. It is not learning a sermon by rote, but mastering the subject.

Another objection, which takes just the opposite ground, is that Extemporary Preaching requires too much time and trouble. Those who raise this objection generally suppose, I find, that the Extemporary Preacher learns his sermon by rote, and delivers it as a player does his part. It is obvious that if this objection is made in good faith, it must be made by those who have themselves such small mental powers that they cannot understand how any one can attain to the faculty of explaining *vivâ voce* a subject he has previously studied and digested, and which he has a strong desire to convey and commend to the minds of others. The objection, however, I believe is only partially made in good faith. Such an objector really does find some difficulty in forming a conception of a mental effort of this kind—no great thing after all, indeed not more than every well-educated youth ought to be capable of making—but he also, and that is probably his chief object, wishes to insinuate that the Extemporary Preacher's motive is vanity, and vanity of such an inordinate and irrational kind, that he will, in order to gratify it, give himself the trouble of learning by heart two sermons every week of his life. If a man could be found who might be able to make such an effort of perseverance and memory, still, I think, he would hardly be disposed to continue it after a few months' experience of the time it required. Besides, if a man were to trust in this way to his memory only, he must occasionally break down in the most complete and distressing manner. This objection is as puerile as the former one. Neither of the two kinds of preaching they suppose at all resembles that which I am endeavoring to recommend in these pages. Still it may be of some use to have made this mention of them; for marking off what is not meant, contributes towards giving a definite idea of what is meant.

33. It is a security against verbal repetitions.

A third objection one hears very frequently urged is, that Extemporary Preaching abounds in repetitions. I dare say a great deal of repetition is heard in the so-called sermons of mere declaimers and extemporary talkers, but it ought never to be heard in those of the Extemporary Preacher. He is a man who knows what sermons ought to be, and takes care that the matter of each of his own shall be arranged on a plan for every part of which there is a good reason. Nothing can be omitted or transposed. This excludes the possibility of repetition. And we may ask, What reason is there for repetitions in religious any more than in political or judicial addresses? Indeed, there is less reason; for an advocate or a parliamentary speaker must often be obliged to speak when more or less unprepared to do so. This can never happen to a preacher. I am writing to educated men, who are too self-respecting and have too much respect for their sacred work, ever to omit the previous consideration of what they shall say from the pulpit. There will be some who will not do this as carefully as it should be done, or who, from a want of skill in composition which nature has denied them the power of acquiring, or from an inability to put any thing, even to their own minds, otherwise than in a confused and illogical manner, will be exposed to this objection; but these are people who would be just as confused, as illogical, and incoherent, and as full of repetitions of ideas, if not of words, in written discourses. I am disposed to think that this objection is frequently made on very insufficient grounds, being merely taken up as the readiest weapon that comes to hand, when the objector for some other reason dislikes either the preacher or Extemporary Preaching.

34. It is too earnest and direct for some hearers.

As this other reason is one that is rather felt than expressed, it results in what I will describe as the tacit objection of those who, not being in religion of a zealous temperament themselves, dislike being brought in contact with the zeal of others. To such persons there is an earnestness and directness in extemporary preaching which is distasteful. But the fault here is not in the preacher, or in the method he adopts. What is really objected to, is what others will regard as one of the peculiar merits of that method.

35. False inferences in favor of reading, from false analogies.

I have seen the practice of reading written sermons defended on the ground that the Preacher is not a debater. True. But are addresses of no kind to be delivered without book except such as are called for in debate? And are we to believe that the practice with respect to Preaching of all Churches in all times, excepting that of our own Church, is wrong? And what is there in exposition, exhortation, rebuke, warning, and the appeals a Minister of the Word must make that renders the reading them from a MS. the most appropriate method of delivering them? It is also said that the Preacher is near of kin to the lecturer on Moral Philosophy, and that as lectures on this subject are generally read; therefore sermons also should be read. No such thing. It might be better if the lecturer were so completely master of his subject as to be able to speak upon it. But there is no analogy between the two. The Preacher is not a lecturer; nor is the lecturer a Preacher. A man may be a very good lecturer on the Exegesis of Scripture, or on Theology, and yet be a very ineffective Preacher.

36. The true Preacher is very different from the popular Preacher.

I wish the kind of Preacher I have in view in this book to be distinguished in as trenchant a manner as possible from what is called the popular Preacher. Many being acquainted only with the latter have a prejudice against extemporary preaching of every kind. I endeavor to describe in these pages the learning, the never-ending study and thought, the style, the aims of the former. The popular Preacher, however, may be described, taking the common type of the class with instances of which most persons are familiar, as one in whom, regarded as a speaker, the gifts of imaginative power and of great command of language have mastered the understanding and the judgment; and whose knowledge seldom makes his hearers aware of their own ignorance. This description of the popular Preacher does not lead us to infer in him the possession of much capacity for doing useful work in the Ministry of the Word. And, as a matter of fact, very little is done, in such a way as to have any permanent effect, by such Preachers. Even those who are themselves of such mental calibre as to admire and run after a popular Preacher of this kind would be more benefited by a wise and well furnished Preacher. These are the very minds that require the discipline of exact thought, and accurate reasoning. Popular sermons full of flights of the imagination, and decked out with brilliancy of language, occupy among the works of the human mind the position the jelly-fish holds in the animal kingdom. Its coloring possesses some attractive brightness; but it is an invertebrate affair, without bone or muscle. As soon as you attempt to handle it, it collapses into nothing. Popular sermons will seldom bear printing. Their appropriate element is the peculiar atmosphere which surrounds the pulpit of the popular Preacher. They cannot be carried away, or turned to any useful purpose. No one expects them to yield meat for the strong man; but neither in truth do they supply much milk for babes. It is hard that the style of Preaching which in its substance, often in its aims, is most unlike this, should suffer in any body's estimation, merely from their both happening to use the same method of delivery.

CHAPTER II.

MY OWN METHOD OF ACQUIRING THE POWER OF PREACHING EX TEMPORE.

1. The method I adopted. How sermons for Extemporary Preaching should be studied and composed.

I WILL now proceed to describe to my younger brethren in the Ministry the method I adopted in carrying out my resolution. It was at the beginning of the year 1854, and I commenced by writing during the week two sermons. Knowing that they were to be preached without the aid of the manuscripts, or even notes, I studied the matter and arrangement of each more carefully than I had ever done before for sermons I had written with the view of their being merely read to the congregation. I was led to do this because I foresaw that confusion of thought and redundancy of matter not properly required by the subject must be avoided, as faults of this kind would very probably confuse me in the pulpit; while nothing could more contribute to aid my memory and smooth my path while speaking than a natural and logical arrangement of all that I had to say. That I might make as sure as possible of this, I divided each discourse into chapters, each chapter being a distinct part of the subject; and each chapter I divided into paragraphs, each paragraph being a distinct step in the treatment of what was the subject of the chapter. To each chapter was prefixed a Roman, to each paragraph an Arabic numeral. Between the paragraphs I left small intervals, in which I wrote, in a few words, a heading of the contents of the paragraph. The headings I afterwards copied on one side of half a sheet of note-paper. This enabled me to see at a glance how I had treated my subject, and to judge more easily than I could do by turning over the pages of the MS. whether my method of treating it was natural and logical. On Saturday I again looked over my two sermons, in doing so, making perhaps more use of the short abstracts than of the complete MSS. And again on the Sunday, I gave the half-hour preceding each service to the final consideration of what I was then about to preach. These two subsequent studies enabled me to make several improvements both in the way of additions and omissions; because what I was endeavoring to do was to form each sermon into a connected and coherent whole, from which every thing must be eliminated that had not a definite purpose. My sermons, then, having been written in the course of the previous week, after much consideration of the subject, and having been again studied on Saturday, and once more referred to before the service on Sunday, the result was, that when I entered the church I almost knew the MS. by heart. The line of argument and every explanation and illustration were distinctly before my mind. In consequence, I did not any where pause for a thought or a word. I had no idea that this was to be regarded as extemporary preaching, yet I was not dissatisfied with it for a beginning. It encouraged me to hope, that though I was only now attempting what I ought to have been taught at school[1] more than twenty years earlier, and though I had no natural command of language, and was besides what is called nervous, and that to a very painful degree, still, that I might at last succeed in acquiring the power of addressing my congregation from the stores of my own mind, which I had become convinced ought to be the practice of every Minister of the Word.

2. Necessity of previous study and composition.

Some of my readers will probably be surprised at finding me entering at all on particulars of this kind. Of course there are many persons who would rather have it supposed that they possess the power of composing and delivering sermons properly by the gift of Nature, or at all events who would rather conceal from the world the method by which they acquired it. But I am not

[1] Boys might readily acquire at school a power which would afterwards become that of speaking in public, by being made to

writing these pages for the perusal of those, if there be any such persons, upon whom Nature has bestowed this gift. I have, however, little belief in orators of any kind, and above all of good preachers, by the mere grace of Nature. A man does not even become a mob-orator without practice. We certainly do not hear of any great orator ever having found himself in ready-made possession of his power of skilfully manipulating, if I may so speak, thought and language; but we know that he attained to it by laborious study and long practice. Not but that we may find many who have a kind of natural fluency; but I am very far from attaching much value to this, taken merely by itself, whether it be a natural gift or an acquired power. What I am recommending is, to use, if you have it, or to acquire, if you have it not, the power of delivering fluently and properly a sermon properly composed by yourself: and to compose a sermon properly does not come by the gift of Nature. It is not the result of an intuitive process, but of study, knowledge, reflection. A man must collect his materials; he must be able to judge of the value and use of these materials; and he must learn how to deal with them and arrange them. I do not believe that there is any royal road to the accomplishment of these things, any

give the substance of their written themes or essays *vivâ voce*, and in the same way to give an account of what they may have been translating or reading.

more than there is to the acquisition of any thing else that is worth having. Some, of course, have a greater aptitude for this work than others, but that is all that can be said. Energy and perseverance will make ample amends for some deficiency of natural aptitude; and no one need be ashamed of energy and perseverance; without them a natural aptitude for preaching will be of little value to its possessor or to his parishioners. Genius, we all know, is necessary for great eminence in any department of art, or literature, or intellectual work of any kind, but these pages are not written with the slightest idea of their being at all instrumental in producing great eminence in any of those who may read them. Those who have the capacity for becoming greatly eminent will know of themselves, without the assistance of any thing I or others can tell them, in what way to secure that eminence. They will work, and work effectually, without such guidance. My object is to invite the attention of my younger brethren to that which is the subject of these pages; and to show to those who may come to agree with me as to what they ought to do, that they may probably be able to give effect to what they deem their duty in this matter, by following the course I adopted and found tolerably successful. I am not at all prejudiced in favor of my own method. There will be some who at an early period of their lives became habituated to speaking in public, and they may therefore think the method I followed too tedious and laborious. Possibly they may be able to dispense with some of the writing I recommend; but not, I think, with any of the thought and study I recommend. All that I am solicitous about is, that we should see what is our duty as Ministers of the Word, and endeavor to carry it out. If what I am writing should produce such an effect in the minds of some, I am quite content that others should be surprised at my giving myself the trouble to describe what I thought and what I did in this matter.

3. Sermons written for reading proved quite unfit for Extemporary Preaching.

But to return to the method I was pursuing. I went on as I had commenced. Every week I wrote two sermons *in extenso*, after having carefully studied my subjects and arranged the plan of each before sitting down to write. This previous arrangement of plan is necessary, otherwise the probability is, that the sermon will be written without a plan. I never again used an old sermon. I found all I possessed unfit for Extemporary Preaching. The faults which I now saw made them unsuitable for being so used were faults which must have made them difficult for the congregation to have followed with continuous apprehension when read. They were more or less full of irrelevant thoughts, words, and even paragraphs. They were often unprogressive throughout—that is, they did not set out with a distinct purpose to be reached in the end, to which every thing in the course of the sermon was duly and regularly subordinated. They were sometimes very disjointed and unconnected, all the parts not being logically parts of the same whole, but only in juxtaposition; because, as in the game of dominoes, the beginning of a paragraph had been suggested by the close of that which preceded it. They had too little coherence to be lifted off the paper. These, and other faults which had not been observed, or, if observed, had not been corrected when the MSS. were only to be read, became apparent when I looked over them with the view of preaching them extemporarily. This one fact, which I am setting down just as I found it, must alone go some way towards proving the probable inferiority of the method of reading written discourses.

4. Advisable to prepare MSS. for Extemporary Preaching on all Scriptures upon which one would wish to preach.

I soon began to study and compose during the week more than the two sermons necessary for the coming Sunday. I did this designedly, because we all know that a man can get through more work by doing one thing at a time, than by doing several things at the same time; and I thought it proper that I should have sermons of my own carefully studied and composed on every paragraph in the Gospels, the Acts of the Apostles, and the Epistles of doctrinal or practical interest, and on all those chapters of the Old Testament which are read as the first lessons of the Sunday morning and afternoon services throughout the year. I set myself down to this task with the determination to complete it before I began to occupy myself with any thing else. I completed it in a little more than four years, in which time I had composed not far short of five hundred and fifty sermons *in extenso*. Whether I was away from home, or whether I had friends staying with me, I endeavored not to intermit my work entirely. Of course I soon got ahead of what was required for the coming Sunday. Hence it happened that I frequently preached a sermon I had written some months, or even, after a time, that I had written a year or more previously; but as they had all been composed with a view to being used for Extemporary Preaching, I found it as easy to preach those that had been written some months previously as one that had been written during the foregoing week. Having now completed the number of sermons I wished to have by me in writing, I for some time only wrote my MSS. at about half the length that would be required in preaching them; and then, after a time, I wrote only short abstracts on half a sheet of note-paper.

5. Result of twelve years' experience. The Extemporary Preacher will never preach the

Twelve years have now passed since I began to work on this plan, and I have not yet had occasion to preach all the sermons I wrote in these first four years. Some of my MSS. I have used more than once, but practically I have never preached the same sermon twice: for as I never preach without devoting to the subject I am going to preach upon all the attention I can give it, and without mastering all I am going to say upon it, I almost in every case more or less recast the abstract, sometimes completely remodelling it; and as I have long trusted entirely to the moment for the language and the composition of what I have to say, though, after five or six years I may preach from an old text, and may, in preparing for the pulpit on the occasion of my doing so, look over an old MS., it will not be an old sermon that I shall preach, but one that will have the benefit of the study and practice of the five or six intervening years. It would surprise one not acquainted with such matters, how greatly a little increase in one's own knowledge, or a slight change in one's views, or a change in the requirements of the times, or of one's parishioners at the moment, will affect even the form of a discourse, by leading to the introduction of some new ideas, or by making subordinate that which previously held a prominent place, or *vice versâ;* but so it is. Indeed, it can rarely happen that the Extemporary Preacher who attends to his work will preach the same sermon twice; the language of course can never be repeated, for the changes that take place in one's mind, even if in the meantime there has been nothing that might be called mental growth, and the

Same sermon twice.

difference in one's feelings at the moment of preaching, render that impossible. The activity of the imagination and the flow of language are ever varying, as they depend in a great measure on the circumstances of the moment.

6. The chief difficulty is to make the first effort.

Those who are constitutionally shy and nervous, and whose natural defects of this kind have perhaps been increased, as is frequently the case with clergymen, by the habits of a studious life, will find that a very great effort is required for making the first attempt. It is voluntarily submitting oneself to a kind of unseen martyrdom. But the first Sunday will do much towards mitigating these distressing feelings, because it will prove the possibility, where before all was uncertainty, of carrying out one's resolve. That beginning will enable the preacher to feel assured that if he will give himself the same amount of trouble he has just expended in preparing for his first Sunday, he will on subsequent Sundays do at least as well and be as safe from breaking down and hesitation; or rather, he may have reason for hoping that continued practice will give a proportionate increase of confidence, ease, and power. Here, as in so many other things, it is the first step which is the difficult one to take; that once taken, the way is smoothed for all the steps that are to follow. I note this for the encouragement of those who may be thinking of making the attempt. They will find their first effort far less of a failure than they are beforehand disposed to anticipate. This will very much diminish what they may now be supposing will be the mental distress of their subsequent efforts. In some cases, of course, these uncomfortable feelings will only be removed very gradually. Many of the most accustomed speakers have told us that they never rose to speak in public without experiencing sensations of this kind; though, indeed, there must be more reason for their feeling in this way in the contests of public life, than there can be for the minister of the Word, who is only called upon to make a short address to his own friendly congregation on his own familiar subjects. Speaking from my own experience, I must say that this feeling, to a painful degree, may last for several years, and even afterwards may never entirely leave one. But I found, even in my first years of Extemporary Preaching, when it was most troublesome, that it seldom lasted beyond the first few sentences. One soon becomes, from the necessity of having to attend to what he is about, so completely absorbed in his subject, as generally to lose all consciousness even of the presence of the congregation, certainly to lose all consciousness of self. The beginner is obliged to be so intent on his subject, that with him this will frequently be the case. When practice has given him an easier command of himself, he will be able to attend both to his subject and to his congregation at the same time.

7. What feeling harder to bear than the distress of having to speak *ex tempore*.

But I may be asked, Why incur these disagreeable feelings, when they may be escaped by reading your sermons? I reply, that I incurred them because the feelings of humiliation and shame I experienced, as a Minister of the Word, at reading my sermons, were more distressing. The latter were more distressing, because they impelled me to encounter and to continue to bear the former. The feelings that are suggested Sunday after Sunday, and year after year, by the sight of an uninterested, inattentive, and uninstructed congregation, are far more disagreeable. There is absolutely nothing to compensate for these feelings, while you are amply compensated for the former by the consciousness that you are discharging a sacred duty to the best of your ability, and to the ever-increasing benefit of those to whom you have undertaken to minister the Word.

8. In some cases Exposition may be used as training for Extemporary Preaching.

The method by which a man may attempt to acquire the power of Extemporary Preaching will of course depend in a great measure upon the power he has of speaking in public at the time the resolution is made and the attempt commenced. Throughout these pages I am supposing the case, which is that of a large proportion of the Clergy, of a man who has to begin from the beginning, or even from a worse point than the beginning,—that, I mean, at which a man finds himself who has always been in the habit of reading his discourses, all the while living a somewhat retired and studious life. Such a person comes to have a profound distrust of himself, and looks upon the demands that Extemporary Preaching will make upon him as impossibilities in his case: he feels himself utterly incapable of complying with them. There are many such, and for them mainly I am writing. But there are others, who have made at the University or elsewhere some attempts to speak in public, and found them not altogether unsuccessful; and others, again, who are conscious of possessing some natural powers of this kind. These persons will probably be disposed to adopt some easier and shorter method than the one I am recommending. The following anecdote, which describes a case I am acquainted with, gives one of these other methods. A Clergyman, not long after his arrival in the parish of which he had recently become the Incumbent, was making one of his first rounds of pastoral visits. On entering the house of a petty shopkeeper, he expressed some regret at not having seen the man at church on the previous Sunday. The man replied, that it was true; he had not been at the church; and it was not his habit to be there on Sunday, for he was a Dissenter. The Clergyman repeated his expressions of regret, and asked the man why he was a Dissenter. The man replied, that as the reason was asked, he would unreservedly give it. In the Dissenters' chapels, he said, the Minister always addressed the congregation from what was in his own mind; and what the Minister said was said in such a manner that it was understood by the people, and moved their hearts. The case, however, was very different in the church. There, the Minister, although they were told that he spent many years at school and the University, and that he was a very learned man, was unable, from his own mind, to say any thing to his people; and what he read to them was seldom understood by them, and did not come home to their hearts. And their conclusion was, that they could not believe that God's Spirit was with the Church-Minister, to guide him in what he was reading, and to aid him in reaching their hearts. This statement of the reason which had induced several of his parishioners to forsake the church for the chapel, the Clergyman found himself quite unable to answer. It is true that the argument it contains does not at every point hold water; but it would have been impossible to have answered it satisfactorily to the small tradesman, for after all there was in it a great deal of solid truth. This the Clergyman felt strongly. Here was a cause of weakness to the Church, and a reproach to it which was very discreditable to the Clergy. The more he thought of what the man had said, the more clearly he saw that there was but one way of replying to it, and that was by doing what he was told the Clergy had not the power to do. He decided at once what he would do. He had never spoken in public, but he determined immediately to acquire the power of doing so. He was aware that he possessed some natural aptitude for speaking, and he therefore resolved to commence forthwith the following plan. On the ensuing Sunday he took the Bible up into the pulpit, opened it at the first chapter of St. Matthew's Gospel, and announced to the congregation that it was his intention to expound continuously the whole of that Gospel. He was sure that he would have something to say upon every paragraph, and that he would be able to say it; and he trusted that, as he went on, he would find that he required less and less of the text for his half-hour's exposition. He was not disappointed. Before he got through St. Matthew's Gospel, he found himself able to preach from no more of the text than he would have required formerly for one of his written sermons. The objection of the petty tradesman and of those who reasoned like him was completely met, and they returned, some altogether and some in part, to the Church they had forsaken. Here was a great advantage gained. But I must remind my readers that only a part of what I am recommending in these pages was accomplished.

This Clergyman had acquired, and on very easy terms, the power of preaching in the way which alone can secure the attention and respect of ordinary congregations, and which has, besides, other advantages; but he had done, in doing this, nothing to enrich the matter, to enlarge the views, to strengthen the reasoning, and to improve the arrangement and style of what he said. Let us suppose that every thing of this kind was added in time; for, if not, then the petty tradesman and his fellow-seceders did not gain much more from the sermons of the parish church to which they had returned, than they might have gained from those they would have heard at the chapel they had been induced to abandon. How a thing is said, signifies much; but what it is that is said, signifies more.

9. Reflections and hints the actual practice of Extemporary Preaching suggested. The years 1854, 1855, 1856.

I was in the habit for several years of committing to paper any thoughts which the services of the Sunday, and particularly the sermons, had suggested. The object of this practice was, to preserve any thing that occurred to me, and which I thought it might be of use to remember. A selection from these memoranda, it now appears to me, might have, for those of my readers who may be disposed to give my recommendations a trial, some little interest, perhaps even some little advantage. I will therefore select a few for their perusal. The entries for the first year, 1854, have been lost. In 1855, those that express a sense of slowness of advance, sometimes of no advance at all, are frequent; but I do not find one that presents any indication of my having ever from the first wavered in my resolution, or of my having been dissatisfied either with the amount of work it imposed upon me in these first years, or with the abandonment it necessitated of my former pursuits. At that time the labor was great and the apparent fruits were but slight; this, however, never discouraged me.

In 1856 I find, among many I omit, the following entries:—

Jan. 29.—I am now speaking with less preparation, and yet with more ease than I did a year ago. I must therefore endeavor to be on my guard against falling into any thing like slovenly fluency. By careful attention, I suppose, the habit of speaking with clearness and accuracy may be attained with as much certainty as any other habit.

March 23.—Of late I have advanced very slowly, if at all. But I remember that, as the advantage of being able to discharge one's duty in the pulpit properly is great, so the difficulty of acquiring the power of doing it must be expected to be proportionately great.

"Nil sine magno
Vita labore dedit mortalibus."

Aug. 31.—I find that, next to a good subject well prepared, what sets one most at ease, is a good congregation. A small, inattentive congregation depresses. It implies that the service, of which the exposition of the Word is an important part, has failed, as conducted by the Minister, to awaken interest. This want of interest in the congregation reacts upon him who is more or less the cause of it. A good congregation, for the opposite reason (for the feeling of interest in what is going on is very infectious), gives wings to the spirit of the preacher. It contributes much towards loosening his tongue and giving him freedom of speech.

Oct. 26.—I felt sure to-day that the attention which must be given to sermons intended for Extemporary Preaching, such as I have been obliged to give to mine for now more than two years, must improve a Minister of the Word in sermon-writing.

Nov. 16.—I begin to feel the good effect of attending to what is passing in the minds of the congregation. The speaker is aroused by seeing or feeling that the minds of his hearers are in contact with his own mind. This is a stimulus to thought and expression of which I knew nothing while I read my sermons.

10. 1857. *Jan.* 4.—I was told to-day by one of my most intelligent parishioners, that the congregation were, as far as he knew, without an exception, in

favor of my having abandoned the practice of reading my sermons, and adopted that of preaching them extemporarily. As to my own feelings, though not altogether dissatisfied with my progress, I am very far indeed removed from being satisfied with my performance. I had much to unlearn as well as much to learn, and my progress is very slow; I have however, no thought of abandoning the attempt I am making.

Feb. 8.—What I say is beginning to be better than what I am capable of writing; it is much better put. It was so to-day.

Feb. 15.—I find that the more entirely I trust to the moment for composition, the more completely my subject gets possession of me. This, I think I may take for granted, makes one's speaking more natural and forcible, for it then becomes the expression of the present thought.

March 8.—Preached to-day from a MS. I had written a year and a half ago. In studying it for the pulpit I made great alterations in it. This goes some way towards proving to me that I can write a better sermon now than I could then.

March 22.—In the morning I did badly, though I had thought I had a good MS. to preach from. In the evening I did better, though I had thought that my MS. was very inferior to that used in the morning. In speaking, one's powers vary very much, in accordance with the circumstances of the moment, though sometimes not in the manner one would have supposed beforehand; for one is often able to throw off completely the feelings and thoughts which up to the moment of speaking would obstinately retain possession of the mind.

March 29.—I felt to-day that I was now able to preach without a written preparation.

May 3.—I gave, instead of a sermon, an exposition this afternoon. I became conscious of difficulties and faults peculiar to this form of discourse. In an exposition I see care must be taken to prevent its becoming fragmentary. The way in which the paragraphs, or the consideration of the successive particulars, are connected must be attended to. The repetition of the same connecting phrases must be avoided. Oneness of purpose in all that is said, from the difficulty of securing it in an exposition, ought to be kept in view as an especial aim.

May 10.—I made very little use of my MS. this morning. It was almost useless, plainly because I had not attained to sufficiently clear ideas upon my subject at the time I wrote the MS. This shows that to write in haste—almost, as is sometimes done, against time,—it is not only to waste your labor, but it is something still worse; for it is doing what it is probable may confuse you, when you attempt to preach what you wrote without a proper mastery of your subject, or at inauspicious moments.

May 17.—The Minister of the Word must remember that to speak persuasively is an important part of his work. To have a large and attentive congregation is not a bad proof, though of course not a conclusive one, that he has attained to this power.

May 31.—I found this morning that I could not interest myself in my work, or exert myself; consequently I preached in a slovenly and perfunctory manner. I was rather going over so much ground, than endeavoring to implant certain ideas and awaken certain feelings in the minds of the people before me.

July 5.—To look the congregation in the face is often both a stimulus to the speaker and a guide to him in the treatment of his subject. It tells him whether he is understood, and whether he should drop, or continue to dwell a little longer on what he is speaking about.

Aug. 30.—I felt to-day that I had more complete command of my faculties than usual. I traced this plainly to the mentally invigorating effects of having been travelling about for the preceding month. The great variety of minds, just like the variety of natural scenes and objects one meets with in travelling, refreshes and strengthens.

Oct. 18.—One of the great advantages a speaker has over a reader, is, that he has grasped his whole subject, and sets it before his mind's eye; he is therefore able, as he goes on, to give its proper breadth and color to each part. He works up to and makes his points. The reader must confine himself to what he has before him, and so cannot do these things.

Nov. 8.—I felt something to-day of the hearts and minds of the people I was addressing. I was conscious that their thought and feeling were aroused. I seemed to myself to be giving expression to their thought and feeling. This *rapport* between the speaker and his hearers is necessary. Their thoughts and feelings are partly to be read in their faces, and partly to be divined. To keep oneself in this way in sympathy with one's hearers, is utterly to repudiate the pestilential idea of oratorical display. It is the substitution of the thought of one's audience for the thought of oneself.

Nov. 15.—The preacher should begin by planting his subject in the minds of the congregation. He should do this in such a way as, if possible, to interest them, and set them thinking upon it. They will then go along with the speaker, and be more disposed to adopt his thoughts and feelings. If they are themselves thinking on the subject, he will appear to be giving utterance to their thoughts and feelings.

Dec. 25. Christmas Day.—I heard a young Extemporary Preacher in Ipswich this afternoon. I wished I could have got hold of him, and made him understand that what he wanted was some years of hard study, both thought and reading, to enable him to have something to say that would be worth hearing. He is evidently not aware of the vast difference between saying something, and having something to say. His efforts were not directed to any definite purpose. He made no points. His sermon, if it could be so called, was one dead level of religious common-places.

Dec. 27.—While preaching, my mind now is never occupied about the language I am using, further than to avoid words which would be unintelligible to the rural poor. As one's object is to be understood, to move, and to persuade, one ought to be careful to say nothing but what may be readily followed and taken in by the present congregation. And having ceased to be occupied with the language I use, I can attend more closely to reasoning out and illustrating the point before me.

I have now completed the fourth year of practice 11.
in Extemporary Preaching. Whatever else might have been done with this long period of my working life, I am not dissatisfied with having devoted it to this object. I say this as a Minister of the Word; though possibly I could not, under any circumstances, have employed the time to better purpose. It would, however, have been far better had I begun to practise speaking in public twenty years earlier.

Throughout this year there are no entries of discontent at slowness of progress, but there are some of an opposite character.

I find in this year the following entries without date:—

There are three kinds of material for Extemporary Speaking—Reasoning, Feeling, and Imagination. The first care of the Extemporary Preacher must be to have each of these at command. In the next place, he must be able to clothe in appropriate language what each supplies. Lastly, he must have judgment to know when to use and how much to use of each. These three materials of speaking must be used as different colored threads would be used in a cloth of fair design. Each must always be in hand for use, ready to be taken up and laid down as required. Sometimes the three will be used in the same paragraph. Sometimes, Reasoning, Feeling, or Imagination will be indicated in the use of a single word.

One of the great advantages of Extemporary Preaching is that it obliges the preacher to understand to some extent what he is speaking about. What he understands, there is some prospect of his being able to make intelligible to his congregation.

The matter of what a man says cannot be better than his knowledge and his logic. This is why the ordinary run of popular preachers have no weight at all in the world. They must improve their logic, and increase their knowledge.

1858. *Jan.* 10.—I was very much dissatisfied 12.
with myself this afternoon. I did badly because I had not clearly made out to myself beforehand a part of my argument.

Feb. 14.—Lately I have found myself so entirely absorbed by my subject as to forget the presence of my hearers. This is a mistake and must be guarded against. The speaker ought never to lose sight of the way in which his audience is regarding his subject, and what he is saying of it.

April 18.—For the first time I used a MS. from which I had already preached. It was one that had been written and used at the beginning of 1854. I find that I have very much advanced beyond what I was then capable of doing. The old MS. proved almost useless. I recast the whole of it. Nothing of the kind would have been done under the system of reading. I should not have outgrown a MS. in four years; or, if I had, I should hardly have noticed it, when nothing was to be done but read what was already prepared. The having to master, and construct in the mind what was to be said, showed that something better could now be done than had been done in 1854.

May 9.—I still have nearly one hundred unused MSS., but used to-day, instead of taking two of these, two that I had written and used four years ago. This is good practice, to discover faults, and correct them; and, in consequence of having increased and more digested one's knowledge and enlarged one's experience of what is required in preaching, to remodel an old MS. This accustoms one never to use one's materials without thought and understanding.

July 18.—I find that in preaching there is always a great difference between my way of treating the beginning and my way of treating the latter part of a sermon. At first I am always more diffuse than I am towards the close. This difference probably arises from a difference in the matter. The beginning of a sermon is generally explanatory; and explanations admit of and almost invite diffuseness. The latter part, however, consists generally of application and exhortation. Diffuseness here would mean dilution and weakness. I also find that diffuseness is far easier than conciseness. Diffuseness does not confuse the speaker, though it may the hearer. The attempt at conciseness has a tendency to confuse the speaker. A well-executed conciseness is a great help, and very pleasing to the hearer.

Sept. 12.—I preached this morning for the first time from a sketch drawn out on one side of half a sheet of note-paper. I had sufficiently studied the subject in my mind.

Oct. 10.—I did badly this morning, because I had not made out my subject distinctly to myself. Defective power of speaking, and insufficient study of what one is to speak about, are two very different things.

Oct. 24.—My powers of extemporary thought are much enlarged. At first, my memory was chiefly exercised. Then, language occupied me much while speaking. Now, neither memory nor language occupy me much. My mind is chiefly occupied with seeking for arguments and illustrations, and arranging what I have to say. My practice in Extemporary Preaching has convinced me of the duality of the mind—or rather that the mind is capable of doing two things at the same moment. While I am speaking,—which is one operation, for it is the clothing of thought in language,—I am always thinking of what is coming, sometimes very intently; or of the congregation, of how they will understand and receive what I am saying. Whether these two operations are performed simultaneously by the same organ, or by two distinct yet connected organs, like the two eyes, or the two ears, is a question which I suppose admits of discussion. If the two organs are distinct, they may be so in the fashion of the two hands or the two feet, which are capable of acting simultaneously either for a conjoint purpose, or each for a separate purpose of its own. Or the rapidity of thought may be so great as to dispense apparently with time, and thus to preclude the thinker from distinguishing between the laying down of one subject and the taking up of another. The attention given to the two subjects may in reality be not simultaneous, but consecutive; we may, however, be incapable of observing the consecutiveness of the second act of attention to the first. I would illustrate this supposition by the familiar instance of a long and eventful dream being comprised in the instantaneous act of waking, when a noise or a word has been the cause of the sleeper's having been aroused, and his whole dream was suggested by the very noise or word that awoke him.

Dec. 26.—I have frequently of late preached without any written study, except a few headings set down in a few lines.

I close this year with the entry, that I believe I have during the year improved in preaching, but that I can hardly say that I have made any approaches towards my ideal of a preacher. My imaginative powers generally appear to me to be paralyzed when I am in the pulpit. My reasoning powers are not affected in this way.

13. 1859.—I had now entirely ceased to write sermons *in extenso*. Seven years have since passed, and during that time I have never had occasion to do more than

set down a few short notes, that I might be able to judge of the plan of what I was about to say; and that no part of it,—as must sometimes be the case if no memoranda are made,—might slip out of my mind, and be lost.

CHAPTER III.

SOME REMARKS ON THE COMPOSITION OF SERMONS.

1. Composition of sermons—their effectiveness depends upon it.

I NOW proceed to say something on a subject to which passing references have frequently been made in the foregoing pages—that of the Composition of Sermons. Upon this depends not only the effectiveness of sermons, but also the very power of preaching them effectively. This is true of them even when addressed to the ignorant and uncultivated, who are more impressed by what they hear, understand it more readily, and are able to carry more of it away when the plain natural rules of composition are observed.

2. They must, first of all, be vertebrate compositions.

The first and most essential principle is, that a sermon must be a vertebrate composition. It must have a vertebral column—a back-bone. When this has been secured, other things may be attended to; and just as the higher vertebrate animals have appendages in the shape of limbs, so may this vertebrate composition—a sermon—be the better for an appendage or two. You may depart occasionally from the direct line of the column of construction to append here what may serve as a leg, to give the body of the discourse as it were a little movement, and here what may serve as an arm, to smite the wrong-doer, or to raise the distressed in mind, body, or estate. But these must grow naturally from it, and their use must be obvious. They will give to what is being said motion and action; but the vertebral column itself is the body and substance of the sermon: these additions are the means it uses for effecting its immediate objects.

Sometimes we hear of a speaker having lost the thread of his discourse; sometimes also we hear an Extemporary Preacher accused of having repeated himself. Here we have an accident and a fault, both of which may be avoided by the observance of the rule I have just laid down; for if his sermon be so composed, the preacher must begin at the beginning and go on to the end. What he has to say will then not admit of his doubling back. He will always know just where he is, what he has said, and what he has still to say.

3. To be regarded as works of art of a high order

But speaking in this way of the composition of sermons, suggests the objection that it would give them an artificial character. We must distinguish between what has an artificial character and what is a work of art, which every sermon ought to be, in the sense in which the building itself in which the sermon is delivered is, or a statue, or a picture. Indeed, there is a sense in which the works of nature, as for instance, the terrestrial landscape, the starry firmament, a flower, a leaf, a tree, an animal, the human face, the human figure, are, just like the works of man, works of art, although the terms are commonly used in opposition to each other. The difference between them is, that the latter are the works of a human, and the former of a Divine Artist. What brings any thing under this category, is, that it is conceived and executed with reference to certain principles of proportion, contrast, form, color, and greater or less prominence of certain parts. Conformity in each instance to the principles which that particular kind of work requires, makes the thing done suitable for its purpose, and also makes it a work of art. All this applies strictly to sermons, which, as they are addressed to the understanding and feelings, do in truth occupy a very high place among works of art.

4. Must have unity of purpose.

But I proceed with the remarks I have to make on their composition. No great effect can be produced on the mind and feelings by what is confused and indistinct, and wanting in directness and intelligibility. A man who is unacquainted with, or careless about what are the rules of art belonging to this subject, will sometimes begin an argument and then interrupt himself with some irrelevant considerations. An incomplete argument, or an argument thus broken into pieces, cannot have so much force as it would have had if it had been managed in a more workmanlike manner. An analogous fault, equally or even more inartistic, is to introduce any thing that will produce a different effect from that at which the preacher is or should be aiming, either as the object of his whole sermon or of that particular part of it where the discordant thought or feeling is suggested. He ought not to use so much as a word which would divert the attention of his congregation from his object, by suggesting an irrelevant or superfluous idea. All the powers of thought and feeling both in himself and in his audience, should be made to converge on the present object. This is what we do in conversation. A preacher who understands how his purpose is to be effected will do the same in the pulpit. Matter and words that are irrelevant or superfluous are objectionable in a sermon for the same reasons for which any thing of the same description would be objectionable in a poem, statue, picture, or any other work of art. The difference is, that in such a work as a picture or statue, the whole being taken in by the eye at a glance, if there be any thing irrelevant or superfluous, it is detected instantly; but a sermon, before judgment can be passed on it, requires half an hour's attention and a knowledge of what is really beside its purpose and aim. This implies in the hearer an amount of knowledge which many persons do not possess, and an amount of attention which few persons are disposed to give. Such people will generally allow to pass unnoticed much that may be at discord with and destructive of the effect the sermon should have been intended to produce. Still, even in their cases, the effectiveness of a sermon would be very much increased by a diminution of these faults.

5. What better in sermons than natural eloquence.

Another objection, besides that which mistakes conformity to the rules of art for an artificial character, may be made to the more measured and reasoned kind of speaking which may be expected from the adoption of my recommendations as to regular study and careful composition previous to delivery: it may be said this cannot produce any thing at all resembling true natural eloquence. But may it not produce something much better, and much more suited to the pulpit? We can imagine what would be the effect on the mind, of hearing twice every Sunday, for half an hour at a time, bursts of true natural eloquence. It would become tedious, perhaps insufferable. Accuracy and variety of knowledge, and thoughtfulness in the man one has to hear so frequently, are better than what is meant by true natural eloquence, which is generally accompanied with more or less of ignorance, with want of balance, want of breadth of view and of profundity, and of connectedness and of distinctness of object. These are excellences which can be attained only by patient thought and study.

6. Respective claims of ordinary phraseology and that of our English Bible.

In sermon-writing and preaching a question sometimes arises, as to the most appropriate language. As it is the somewhat archaic character of the language of our English Bible and of our Book of Common Prayer which gives rise to this question, it is evident that whatever difficulties it contains are peculiar among public speakers to the preacher. Some would solve the question by cutting the knot. They say, "Archaic language is unfit for the purposes of the preacher, as it would be for the purposes of any other speaker. Speakers, of whatever kind they may be, should use the language of the day—it must be the language which is most readily understood; and to be readily understood is the object of all speakers." These persons mean that they would have the language of our English Bible and Book of Common Prayer dropped in the pulpit, and the language of the literature of the day adopted in its place. This solution, however, of the question is dictated rather by an exaggeration of the common-sense view of the matter, than by considerations of good taste, or of what would produce the best effect on the minds of the congregation. An instance will perhaps show this better than an argument. A preacher who some years ago was of some note in a country town where he held a benefice, but was afterwards the minister of a more critical congregation elsewhere, agreed with those whose opinion I have just quoted; and once gave (it was his ordinary style of language) the following illustration of the practice of using modern phraseology in sermons. His subject was, "The Children of Light," and his object at the moment was to convey the idea that they are the recipients of light. With this in view he said, "Brethren, to use a philosophic" (he meant a scientific) "term, you are photogenic." The word was taken from the walls of a lucifer-match manufactory in Mile End, which is seen from the Great Eastern Railway; where, however, whether correctly or not, it means exactly the reverse of what the preacher supposed, being applied there to the production, not the reception of light. It is obvious that the use in the pulpit of such fire-new, and would-be scientific, terms as the above, even when applied with perfect correctness, can only be justified by necessity. They jar too much on the ears of educated hearers. If the object be to connect the pulpit as closely as possible with the facts and thoughts of the present day, the object is a most proper one; and the means for doing this which language supplies are not to be neglected; but excess is possible in the use of these means, as in most other things, and ought to be guarded against.

The opposite extreme, that of the preacher confining himself exclusively to the language of our English Bible, is also to be avoided. 7. The effect of this is to take the hearer out of the living realities of the actual world, and to transport him to a region of shadows; for such are words and phrases which are no longer in common use: life has departed from them. The discrepancy between ordinary language and that of the Authorized Version is rapidly increasing; the time therefore cannot be very distant when the bad effect of preaching in the language of the latter will be generally obvious. In the mean time, judgment, good taste, and a common-sense view of the requirements of what we have to speak about, must determine for the preacher in what way he can most effectively express his meaning. Some when wishing to inculcate the practice of "every virtue" would urge the hearer in Biblical phrase "to fulfil all righteousness." Something may be objected to either phrase—at all events it may be said of the latter that the idea it calls up is faint, and not precisely what the preacher wishes to convey. One might hesitate between the Holy Spirit and Holy Ghost, feeling that the latter name is becoming obsolete, and that the former awakens more thought, because to our ears more instinct with meaning. Trespasses and transgressions are words which have almost ceased to appeal to the conscience.

Naughtiness is no longer applied to the delinquencies of grown-up persons.

8. But that multitudes of Biblical words and phrases are thus more or less obsolete is not all; there is also the fact that a great deal of what the preacher has to say cannot be expressed at all, or only very imperfectly, in Biblical phraseology. One almost shrinks from mentioning in the pulpit any place—as, for instance, Paris or New York—the name of which does not occur in the Bible: but this is false taste, and is wrong.

9. Our rule then should be to say whatever ought to be said, on every subject that comes before us in the Ministry of the Word, in the most distinct, direct, and intelligible way; not fearing to use modern phraseology, if it will bring our meaning more forcibly home to the understandings of our congregations than Biblical phraseology would. But at the same time we need not avoid, I would rather say we ought to prefer, Biblical phraseology wherever it can be used without detriment to the effectiveness of what we are desirous of saying. Its use will have this advantage, that it will contribute to invest our discourse with something of a sacred character by connecting it with the source from whence it derives its inspiration. While, however, we do this, we must be careful not to do it to such an extent as to invest our discourse with an unreal and conventional character, as if it were all about matters

that men had ceased to think or to talk about; for if we do not speak in the language in which men think, what we say will not come home to their understandings or their feelings.

10. Openings of sermons will generally be composed last.

The two most important, and at the same time the most difficult, sentences in a sermon are the first and the last. Of these the last is the more difficult of the two. The first will frequently supply the key-note to all that is to follow; while it suggests the object of the discourse, or brings at once into prominency some fact or thought which is material to the Preacher's purpose, and which he therefore desires that the congregation should bear in mind. The sentence that is to do this in the most appropriate manner for the whole of what is to follow, can seldom be hit upon when one first sits down to write a sermon; but it will always readily present itself to the mind when the whole subject has been completely grasped, and not only its aim, but the way in which each part contributes to that aim, distinctly made out. When all this stands clearly and palpably before the mind's eye, the point from which the preacher is to start will suggest itself. This is so certainly the spontaneous result of knowing what one is about, and has to do, that in Extemporary Preaching the beginning of a sermon may generally be left to the moment of delivery. In actual composition, therefore, the first paragraph will generally be most to the purpose if written last, because it is properly the result of what all the rest happens to be. The preacher will know the precise point from which he is to set out when he knows the exact point he is to make for, and the ground he is to go over.

11. Further remarks on the opening sentence.

Again, it is by no means an invariable rule that the preacher should begin by stating his subject, because if the subject be of such a nature that the congregation will not readily understand or accept it, it is obvious that it may be better to introduce the announcement of it with some argument, or statement, or illustration, that will lead on to it, and dispose the congregation to accept it.

12. Concluding sentence difficult, and of different kinds.

The conclusion, however, of a sermon is perhaps of greater importance and of greater difficulty. Its purpose may be either to sum up in an impressive manner what has gone before, which must be done by recalling as much of it as can be recalled in a few short sentences; or to state forcibly the conclusion of the whole; or to bring all that has been said to bear on the reason and conscience of the hearer. It might appear that it must be easy enough to conclude, because when a speaker has said all that he has to say upon a subject, then he has arrived at the natural end of the matter. It is not so, however, with a sermon. If one were writing a disquisition, or an essay, that would generally be sufficient; but the preacher has furthermore to make the treatment of his subject impressive; he has to put it in such a way that it shall not only convince the reason, but also interest the feelings of the congregation. He has to leave an impression—to interest—to move—to persuade. Hence arises the difficulty of concluding in a satisfactory manner, for it is no easy thing that has to be done, and it has to be done in a few words; and the feeling will often be left on the preacher's mind that the effect of his sermon was short of what it might have been had there been more concentration and power in his conclusion.

Several of Bishop Butler's celebrated fifteen 13.
sermons conclude with some Scripture which more or less embodies his general aim, or recalls his argument. This method has great advantages. It is as it were a summary of one's own sermon in the authoritative language of the Word of God. The mind receives it as a strongly corroborative argument, which produces this effect without its having been directly used, or stated as an argument.

Many of our Lord's parables conclude with in- 14.
stances of the most wonderful condensation combined with exhortation—for example, those of the Good Samaritan, the Pharisee and publican, the unjust steward, the unforgiving servant, the wise and foolish virgins, &c. It will not often perhaps happen that such terminations as these would be suitable to our

sermons, still it would be of use to the preacher to regard them as perfect models which may occasionally be imitated.

15. What to be avoided in conclusions. But whatever be the form of conclusion which a sermon may require, nothing can be more frigid and destructive of effect than the announcement so frequently heard, that it is the conclusion. The "In conclusion," or "Now to conclude," or "Finally," appears generally to bring a feeling of relief both to the Minister and to the congregation; although they are sometimes put in such a way as to imply that it is time alone which is obliging the preacher to end his discourse. The effect of this is very bad.

16. Uniformity of plan to be avoided. How. Announcement of divisions to be avoided. In his commencements and terminations, and the whole construction of his sermons, the preacher must carefully avoid falling into the habitual use of any single plan. Every Sunday, and this for year after year, he has to preach two sermons; how insufferably tedious then will it prove to his auditors, if all his sermons should be constructed alike. This cannot be the case if his plan is always taken from his subject. If this be done, the requisite amount of variety in treatment will be secured. The caution now being given is by no means unnecessary, for one form of the fault is, at all events, very common, that of dividing the subject. Many preachers seem to

think that in a sermon this is a necessity; accordingly every sermon they preach is divided. You will hear again and again in sermon after sermon—"This text has three," or, it may be, "half-a-dozen points." Then they are enunciated and numbered. This is followed by the separate treatment of each. The irksomeness of composing and preaching such sermons must be very great, though as they are the preacher's own work he may be somewhat blind to their dulness; but he ought to consider what must be the effect of two sermons of this kind every Sunday year after year on the minds of educated, and even of uneducated, people. It will often be the case that a text contains two or three statements or particulars, and it may be necessary for the preacher to bear this in mind in treating his subject, and to take them separately; and when he has done with the consideration of the first, to mark the transition to the next in some way, as for instance by saying, "We now pass to the consideration of another point our text contains," or something of this kind, and so on with the rest: but it can very rarely happen that there is any necessity at the commencement of an address of half an hour's duration to enunciate the divisions of the subject. They may, without the preacher's doing this, be marked distinctly enough, if requisite, in the treatment of the subject. The first moments of your address, when you are always listened to attentively, may be much better employed. The old joke against this style of preaching, that there is in it a great deal of carving, but very little meat, is far from being all that can be said against it. Its sameness, its departure from the natural method of treating a subject, the inevitable unmeaningness of many divisions of this kind, present a combination of faults that is quite insufferable.

17. Repetition of ideas to be avoided.

A fault that is very common, but not so obvious as it is common, is that of the repetition of ideas. One who sits down to write without knowing distinctly what he is going to aim at, or the path by which he is to reach his aim, is constantly liable to fall into the fault of reproducing the same thoughts in different words. Sermons of this kind are very wearisome, without the hearer being always able to point out the cause, for it generally happens that one requires, in order to discover what is amiss in such sermons, more than is possessed by most men of the power of analyzing and arranging ideas. This kind of repetition, from its very nature, is more likely to be found in written than in Extemporary Sermons, for in the latter a proper grasp of the subject must be taken, and therefore in its treatment an advance will be made by distinct steps to a distinct end. There are some whose sermons are rather an array of Texts connected in some way or other with their subject, than a discourse upon or a proper treatment of their subject. Their practice is a very simple one.

It is to collect these Texts, and then to enlarge upon them *seriatim*. This is what South tells us the Puritans of his day called "a saving way of Preaching." His own comment on this description of their style being, "that he knew nothing it saved, except the time and thought of the Preacher." In this method repetition of ideas is unavoidable.

18. Exhortation necessary—in what it consists.

Exhortation is a necessary part of a sermon, because the object of preaching is to influence the will. Arguments and demonstrations only affect the reason and the understanding. And though the reason may be thoroughly convinced, the preacher's work is only done in part. He aims at convincing the reason with the ulterior view of regarding such convictions as levers by which he hopes to move the will. He has then to consider how this leverage is to be brought to bear. It can only be done by showing that what has been proved and established is advantageous or disadvantageous to the hearer. And this can only be done by addressing the feelings and sentiments of the congregation; that is, by appealing to their moral sense, to their religious sentiments, to enlightened self-love, to their approval of what is just, and true, and noble, and lovable, to their hopes and fears, to their desires and affections. The attempt in these ways to awaken emotion in the congregation, and so to lead it to accept or reject what reasoning has demonstrated, is properly exhortation.

It is an appeal to their feelings on the subject before them. It is absurd to object to these appeals to the feelings, for if they are not to be made, then there can be no such thing as exhortation; and then there can be no such thing as influencing the will: for reasoning, as a general rule, cannot do it. The will is reached, as nature seems to have intended, through the feelings. The demonstration of one of Euclid's problems convinces the understanding, but, as this is not a subject about which the feelings can be interested, the matter ends when the proof is understood: the will can be in no way affected by that proof. So you may demonstrate the statements that Jesus Christ is the Light of the world, and the Saviour of the world, but you will have done little, as a preacher, till by making men feel that it is for their advantage to receive Him in these capacities, you shall have brought them to wish so to receive Him. To do this you must appeal to their sense of sin, to their desire to be at peace with God, to their gratitude, to their natural approval of all that is pure and holy, and to any other feelings by which you may hope to draw them to desire what you have proved. These appeals are exhortations.

19. Light and shade necessary. The preacher who attends to what he is about will often be reminded by his own preaching, as well as by what he hears from others, that a sermon requires both light and shade. It is a

great fault when every thing from first to last is kept at one uniform level. This, indeed, goes some way towards making what is said unintelligible, except to those who can separate its sense from the form and manner in which it is put. The points towards which one has been working, and the appeals made to the feelings and Christian consciousness of the congregation, and other main parts of the discourse, ought to stand out distinctly from the general level, so that the congregation shall at once understand their importance, and their relation to the other parts. We often, however, hear the same exalted style and the same impressive delivery continued throughout, or the same sobriety of language and calmness of feeling. Both obscure the preacher's meaning by putting the comparatively unimportant parts on the same level as the most important. The Extemporary Preacher is more likely to escape this defect, and it is a very considerable one, than the reader of written sermons, because whatever the former says, he says with a clear conception of its bearing on the rest of his discourse; he will therefore in preaching, just as he would in conversation, emphasize and bring out what he knows ought to be so dealt with: in his case every thing comes fresh from his thoughts and feelings. Invariable rules can hardly be given on this subject. The sense and object in view must in each case point out what ought to be made prominent. Sometimes, though this will not often be the case, the first words of the sermon, as the *Quo usque tandem* of Cicero's first oration against Catiline, will be of this character; and sometimes it will be requisite that the concluding paragraph should be calm and unimpassioned. Any invariable rules on this point are not only impossible, but would be prejudicial if possible, because they would lead to uniformity of treatment, which ought carefully to be avoided in preaching, so often to the same hearers. It would be very tedious and wearisome to the congregation to find the preacher twice every Sunday emphatic by rule in the same parts of his discourse. What he has to attend to is to be emphatic, impressive, or solemn whenever the sense requires it of him. This implies that he must also bear in mind the converse of what has just been said, I mean the necessity of shade as well as of light, of calmness as well as of energy, of deliberateness as well as of rapidity of delivery. And it may not be out of place here to remark, that all this applies not more to the manner in which God's Word is expounded and enforced, than it does to the manner in which it is read, and the Word read occupies a large part in our Liturgy.

20. Correct Emphasis comes naturally in speaking. Difficult in reading.

I will here add a word or two on the subject of Emphasis. In reading the Prayers little or no emphasis is required. My remarks are intended only for Preaching; but still even with this restriction, I cannot make them without some misgivings, knowing that one can hardly make a wrong emphasis, who fully understands and feels what he is saying, and that one who does not, but yet thinks he ought to emphasize the important words, can only be right by accident; and that, therefore, the emphases in which he will happen to be correct will be far outnumbered by those in which he will be mistaken; and often in such a way as to cause a smile. But I overrule my misgivings by the consideration that in Preaching no emphasis is a fault, and wrong emphasis a very great fault; and that in this, as in all other particulars of delivery, we ought to know what is a fault, and avoid it; and what is correct, and endeavor to attain to it. Points of this kind are best explained by examples. The late Archbishop Whately used to make the remark that Clergymen in reading the Ten Commandments, generally emphasize the "not" in the second, the third, the sixth, and the four following Commandments. This he considered wrong, on the ground that the question is not, whether the subject-matter of these commandments respectively is forbidden, or enjoined. There is no question on that point. They are all obviously and necessarily prohibitions. The question is, what is the thing forbidden? That is what the mind is listening for; and so that is what in each case ought to be made clear and unmistakable by being emphasized. For instance, "making graven images," "taking God's name in vain," "murder," "committing adultery," "stealing," &c. The "nots" are not to be slurred over, but they are not the emphatic words. I think one has only to read the 18th verse of the xix. ch. of St. Matthew's Gospel to be convinced of the justice of this comment. I lately heard an elderly Clergyman reading this part of the Ante-Communion Service, and throughout he emphasized the "Thou" of each Commandment in a manner the effect of which, as it went on accumulating, might, in some of the congregation, have disturbed the reverential feeling proper to tho occasion. This mistake could not have been made designedly, for if so, it would have implied that the reader was of opinion that all mankind, with the exception of those to whom the Decalogue had been given, were at liberty to blaspheme, murder, steal, etc. The occurrence of such mistakes in the reading of the Ten Commandments, intimates that it is no easy thing for the reader to emphasize correctly. My object is to show the importance of right emphasis. I make no attempt to give rules, because correctness in this matter can only be secured when the reader is able to realize to his mind, at the instant of uttering the words, all their meaning, purpose, and connection. This is often difficult in itself, and the difficulty is greatly increased in the case of the reader, by the fact that what he has to do is a direct inversion of the natural order of things in this matter. The natural order is to have the feeling and the meaning in the mind first, and then to seek for words by which utterance may be given them; whereas the reader has the words presented to him first, and then has to find what they mean.

I would give from the *Te Deum* the short 21
sentence "We believe that Thou shalt come to be our Judge," as an instance of the great facility with which false emphases may be made, and of the Protean effects, upon what we are reading, of such mistakes. We have here, if we omit the conjunction "that," and regard "to be" as a single word, a sentence of eight words, susceptible of eight distinct meanings; each of these eight meanings being brought out solely and entirely by the position of the emphasis; for in every case the words used would be the same. It may be worth while to spend a few moments in observing this instance of the transforming effect of emphasis. If the first word, "we," be emphasized, it implies that the meaning of the declaration is, that others do not believe this proposition, but we do. The whole sentence then becomes an answer to the question, who believes it? We do. If "believe" be emphasized, it implies that our state of mind with respect to the statement made, is not that of inquiry, or of acquiescence, or of affirmation, etc., but of belief, and the sentence becomes a reply to the question, What is our state of mind with respect to this proposition? If

"Thou" be emphasized, its meaning becomes that we believe Jesus Christ to be the coming Judge; and it is a reply to the question, Who is to be the coming Judge? If "shalt," its meaning is that what we affirm is irrevocably fixed, and it becomes a reply to the question, Whether we are absolutely certain on this point? If "come," it means that Jesus Christ is not here now in a visible bodily form, but that He will reappear in that form, and it is a reply to the question, Will Jesus Christ ever leave heaven, and return again to earth? If "to be," its meaning is that His being our Judge will not be an accidental, or undesigned result of His coming, but its very intended purpose. If "our," its meaning is that whoever may be the judge of Turks, infidels, and heretics, Jesus Christ is He by whom we shall be judged. If "Judge," its meaning is that at His second coming, His character will be that of a Judge. Now here are eight meanings, any one of which, if brought out by emphasis, will occupy the mind, and so hinder the perception of the other seven. The inference I would draw from this in connection with my present subject, is, that it must be very difficult indeed for one who reads his sermons to make correct emphases. It generally happens, which is just what might be expected, that the reader of sermons makes little or no use of emphasis; and this may be one cause of the complaint of the dulness of sermons delivered in this manner. The least inattention to what is being read, or the preoccupation of the reader's attention by his MS., which is virtually inattention to his subject, must result in a great many neglected, and a great many wrong emphases. In conversation, the most illiterate clown is not guilty of these faults, because his words are the expression of his present thought and feeling. The same remark, though not quite to the same extent, may be made of the Extemporary Preacher.

CHAPTER IV.

SOME REMARKS ON THE AIMS AND SUBJECTS OF SERMONS.

1. Subjects and aims of Modern Preaching. Several epochs in the history of the Church. Each has its own distinctive character.

I NOW come to another part of my undertaking, that of the subjects and aims of the modern preacher. He will do well to consider, that though ultimately, and in their simplest expression, the subjects and aims of the preacher must always be the same, yet that they bear such a relation to the times that he who does not take that relation into account will in a great measure in his preaching beat the air. The Christian Church has advanced through several epochs, each characterized by very distinct features of its own. We find the first age marked by great freedom and variety, as well as freshness and depth of feeling and thought. Then comes an age of hard doctrinal controversy. In the Mediæval Church we find an honest formalism and religious submission to authority. At the time of the Reformation men are debating eagerly the question of the grounds of acceptance, whether the individual is to depend on the authority of the Church, or on the simple Word, and the action of the Divine Spirit on his own heart. At the present day the characteristics of all former epochs appear to be in conflict. And out of this conflict there appears to be rising, coming as well from the side of the laity as of the Clergy, a sense of the necessity of insisting on our right to use "the liberty wherewith Christ has made us free," which prompts men to look every where for what is good and true, and to approve it wherever found; and which is disposed to make the main feature of religion the imitation of Christ; and the main feature of that imitation the effort, in accordance with His example, to do good; and which sets above all precepts that one which bids us "be perfect, even as our Father in heaven is perfect," that is, to be true, and just, and holy, and loving. And so it was with the Old Dispensation. As its history advanced, new epochs opened upon it. Prayer and thanksgiving became a higher service than that of sacrifices. The moral law was clearly distinguished from and elevated above the ceremonial. The value of contrition and repentance was revealed. Messianic anticipations became distinctly a refuge from the distresses and perplexities of the present. It is evident then that the preacher ought to address himself to the feelings, the wants, the mental movements of his time, not because they are necessarily right in every particular, but because there must be reason for their existence; and it is his business not to ignore or to denounce that reason, but to consider it, and to find how much truth there is in what is acting widely and deeply on the feelings and minds of men. To do otherwise,—to live in a bygone world, or in a world of his own,—is to render his ministry of the Word useless.

2. The character of the age must be attended to. The safeguard provided against carrying this to an extreme.

The remark readily suggests itself, that this attention to the spirit and wants of the times may be carried too far; for instance, in an age of controversy one may be occupied too much with controversies, and acquire too controversial a spirit. But in an age of controversies, controversy must be attended to: it is the work of the age. Or again, in an age when religious formalism and submission to authority are in the main alone possible, one may exaggerate what are the necessities of the age; but if these are the necessities of the age, the preacher ought to understand their necessity and uphold them. I am supposing a man of good judgment, and of such an amount of knowledge as may be expected in a Minister of the Word, for without them he will be liable in any question he may have to consider to be carried to faulty extremes. The preacher, however, has a safeguard which will never fail him, and that safeguard is, that he must ever speak in accordance with the Spirit of Christ, remembering that, as the Minister of Christ, he stands in Christ's place.

3. How Christ is all in all in the Word. He must be so to the preacher.

We can see a good reason why the Word, although it had embraced the whole history of the Jewish Church, should end where it does, and should not go on to include the history of the Christian Church subsequent to the Apostles' times, notwithstanding its importance. As what is contained in the Word was to form the subject of the study of God's people, and the subject of the preaching of the Ministers of the Word, it was necessary to confine it to the history of Him who is the Author and Finisher of our Faith,—the Way, the Truth, and the Life. The Messianic anticipations of the Old Testament, in which that Dispensation issues, prepare the way for Him. We then have the picture of His life, and the account of what He taught. Then how He was preached by the Apostles, and His kingdom established. He therefore is the subject of the entire Word. It is not merely that His figure stands forth from it, but that He is the centre to which every thing it contains more or less directly converges. This could not have been so much the case had the Word been made to include the subsequent history of the Church. In that subsequent history, man, with his passions, and follies, and mistakes, is generally more prominent than God. But now the preacher of the Word can hardly misunderstand his subject; or, if he strays from it, he must do so wittingly.

4. It would be mischievous, if it were possible, to revive a bygone epoch.

As the Word, then, now stands, presenting to the preacher's view Jesus Christ and Him only, he must, like the Apostle Paul, be determined in a certain sense to know Him only. But there will be some among both preachers and hearers who will see the great central truths of religion through the light of subsequent portions of the Church's history; for the great epochs of its history do not appear to come utterly to an end, but as it were to live on in the minds and hearts of some here and some there, almost as if all that had taken place since had taught them nothing: for them subsequent history appears to have no existence. So it is in an especial manner with the Mediæval epoch, which in many leading particulars teaches lessons very different from those taught us by the first ages of the Church. Still though the lessons taught by these two ages were so widely different as to be almost contradictory of each other, yet the ideas and practices of each were relatively to their own times equally wise and equally true. Each presents to us truths which after-times ought not to lose sight of, and which may be profitably made use of in other times as occasions may arise, but which it must be futile and mischievous to attempt to reproduce again in their complete form; for having once been displaced by the growth of religious ideas and practices, they can never again possess the whole field: nor is it desirable that they should. For instance, how suited to the times, and therefore how powerful an instrument for subduing and keeping in subjection men's minds, was the imposing ritual of the Mediæval Church, aided by the ministering arts of Architecture, Sculpture, Painting, and Music. How invaluable also for those times was the principle of submission to ecclesiastical authority. And of what great advantage was it that the Church was able to organize society for the work of society wherever the motive or aim of the work was religious, as in founding and maintaining asylums to which in those rough and troublous times the weak, and those weary of the world might retire; and in being the great almoner of society; and in providing a sufficient number of churches and Clergy for the comforting and instruction of the people. The Mediæval Church teaches us that these things were of great value in those times, and so suggests the probability of their being of value, with certain qualifications and adaptations, under the changed circumstances of other times. But while we admit this, we must not forget that the Primitive Church grew and prospered under far more arduous circumstances, without a settled ritual; without the ministering aid of Art; without the subjection of society to ecclesiastical authority; and without the power of organizing society for religious purposes. It worked with other and very different instruments; and of these the same may be said as of the instruments used by the Mediæval Church, that they were the best adapted to their own times; and that with those qualifications, which are necessary if they are applied usefully to altered circumstances, they have a value for all times. And so we might go on through all the epochs of the Church's history. Absolutely then those preachers are wrong who hold up the practices and ideas of any bygone epoch as if they ought to rule the present. Relatively, however, such preachers may be doing a good work, for they are the counterpoise to those who ignore, or misunderstand, or ignorantly decry, the practices and ideas of the past. He alone in this respect will be doing his work properly who shall claim for the Church of to-day the same liberty of action which the Church has used in all anterior epochs; and which, however strenuously resisted, must in every epoch be established eventually; and who, because he understands the spirit of the anterior epochs of the Church's history, and their necessary connection, will, instead of vainly endeavoring to recall men to what has passed away, together with the reason of its existence, confine himself to the advocacy only of what may still be of use in the ideas and practices of the past. To contend for what has become obsolete, because unsuitable to the wants and circumstances of the times, cannot be a means for conveying to men's minds a knowledge of Christ, or of extending His kingdom: it can only obscure the former and limit the latter. It makes men conscious that there is an oppugnance between Him as He is preached to them and what they know, and feel, and desire. Where this is the case, the fault probably is in the preacher. Christ is for all times, as much for the modern as for the Mediæval or the ancient world. Indeed, the modern preacher has an advantage over those of previous ages, inasmuch as he has a more extensive armory of means to choose from; only let him not endeavor to make use of weapons unsuited to the existing condition of the fight.

5. Sermons must not be regarded as Confessions of Faith.

A mistake to which attention may now be directed is that into which preachers fall when they make their sermons too theological. There are some whose discourses consist of dogmatic statements, and again of dogmatic statements perpetually reiterated. Christian doctrine is not to be lost sight of in the pulpit, and on many occasions it must be the direct object of the preacher to enunciate and establish it; but speaking generally this is not his object. His object is precisely that of the prophets of old, and of the Great Master Himself. Let him take the Bible for his guide. His object is to exhort, to warn, to comfort, to instruct, and to do all these on Christian grounds.

We sometimes hear it affirmed, that a sermon ought not to be regarded as the address of a Christian preacher to a Christian congregation unless the doctrine of the Trinity, and also the work of the Second and Third Person of the Trinity in the redemption of man, can be readily collected from its statements. Such opinions as these indicate very little knowledge either of the principles of composition or of the human mind. The principles of composition require that each sermon should have its own subject, and that that subject should be set forth distinctly. It should stand out to the mind, as a well-grown tree does to the eye, clearly defined, with its own stem and its own system of branches; but these people would smother all their trees, as nature sometimes does in the tropical forest, with the same set of overwhelming creepers. We must remember that what the congregation have to judge of is not a single sermon, but a long series of sermons,—to be precise, two sermons preached each Sunday by the same person through many years; and we must consider what would be the effect of the distinctive doctrines of our religion being made a more or less prominent feature in every one of these hundreds of sermons. There is no one but can tell what the effect of it would be upon his own mind. It would be neither attractive nor edifying. Let the preacher, then, recollect, that Confessions of Faith are one thing, and that sermons are another.

But, however, on the other hand, the preacher must take care lest, while avoiding the mistake of being too doctrinal, he fall into the opposite mistake. Sermons cease to be sermons as soon as they lose sight of the Faith. Nothing can be more frigid and soulless, or produce a more disagreeable sense of discord, than the discourses of those who adopt the moral essay and Bridgewater Treatise style of preaching. The preacher must preach the Gospel of Jesus Christ; not only because there is no other subject so deeply and enduringly interesting to man, but because there is no other subject on which he is commissioned to speak. Pulpits are not, and could not be, maintained for any other purpose. When Napoleon I. was told that it was proposed, in arranging the administration of the Neapolitan kingdom, to retain, though on a greatly reduced scale, a Church establishment, on the ground of its utility to literature, he replied, with the sagacity which characterized all his legislative ideas, that that was not a ground upon which any Church establishment, however small, could be maintained; that there was but one ground upon which it could be maintained, which was its utility as an instrument of religious consolation and instruction.

6. Nor, on the other hand, as mere Bridgewater Treatises, or moral essays.

The preacher will have to consider what position he will take up in reference to the increased scientific knowledge, and

7. How the preacher must regard the increased sci-

entific knowledge and the historical and Biblical criticism of the present day.

the more profound Biblical and historical criticism of the present day. Many ignore these matters altogether. This may be done in some rural parishes without any great hurt to the congregation, though never without some damage to the mind of the preacher himself; for these are matters with which he ought to be acquainted, and upon which he ought to have arrived at the best conclusions his opportunities admit of. The question, however, is full of difficulty. Neither scientific nor critical knowledge is within every body's reach. Speaking for myself, I have no fear that the modern advances of science, and the wider spread of scientific knowledge, will weaken men's faith in the Gospel of Jesus Christ. There was a time when it was supposed, and perhaps even with more reason than at present, that the then recent discovery of the laws which regulate the solar system, and the revelations made by the telescope, must have this effect. It was demonstrated that this earth was not the centre either of the sidereal or of the solar system; and it appeared no longer possible to localize either the heaven above or the hell beneath the earth. But I am not aware that any one now finds that his astronomical knowledge indisposes him to Christian belief. With respect to the historical and Biblical criticism of the present day, the result probably will be that it will give us more distinct ideas than we now possess with respect to the religious history and progress of mankind, which is a very different thing from overthrowing religion. Its concern with the Sacred Text is to ascertain its meaning, and to offer us an interpretation of it in harmony with the existing state of knowledge. These interpretations can hardly be hostile to that progressive revelation of Himself which God has ever been making, through patriarchs and prophets; and then through Jesus Christ; and with the enlargement of our knowledge may expand, but cannot diminish. At all events, however, there are two remarks which may be made on this subject with which every body will agree, and which cover some portion of the ground which the question opens up to us. One of these remarks is, that it will very much weaken the influence of the pulpit if it be found to have placed itself in unreasoning antagonism to the science and the criticism of the day; and the other is a warning against the opposite course, that of being over eager to accept as ascertained and established facts matters which have not yet advanced beyond the stage of scientific or critical conjecture.

8. He must consider the change in the relation of the intelligence of the congregation to that of the preacher.

The modern preacher will do well to consider how greatly the relation of the intelligence of congregations to that of preachers differs at the present day from what it was in former times. In some cases this difference is so great that it amounts to a partial inversion. There were times when the Clergy alone were educated. Of those times they were the natural and undisputed intellectual leaders. But now all the upper classes are similarly and equally educated; and, indeed, education has been extended even to the lowest classes of society. And moreover, as the Clergy must devote a large portion of their time to parochial work, there are many of the laity who are able to follow up intellectual pursuits far more thoroughly than is possible for the Clergy.

9. Also the enlargement of the means of instruction.

Simultaneously also with this great alteration in the intellectual position of the laity towards the Clergy, there has been brought about an equally great difference between the relation which the modern pulpit bears to the now existing means of instruction, and that which the Mediæval pulpit bore to what were the means of those days. It almost might be said, that in those times the pulpit stood alone as the only means of instruction; but in these days the press has become far more widely used, and far more powerful than the pulpit. These are facts which are most material to any profitable consideration on the subject of preaching.

10. These changes suggest the justice of some of the

At all events, they at once oblige us to acknowledge that there may be some justice in the reiterated complaints we hear from the more highly-cultivated portion of the laity of the dulness and unprofitableness of the generality of modern sermons. Their attainments in knowledge, and the thought they have bestowed on that knowledge, are in advance of the knowledge and thought which perhaps the majority of modern sermons exhibit. If this be so, and few I believe are disposed to dispute it, there can be but one way of meeting the complaint, and that is by our paying more attention to preaching; by which I mean, that we must endeavor to attain to fuller and wider knowledge of the subjects upon which we have to speak, and to a more effective and better way of saying what we have to say. In other words, what we have to do is, I think, what it is the object of this little work to recommend. The knowledge and practice I am speaking of as requisite, cannot, I know, be secured without many years of study; but this is not more than men give in every profession and calling to what is to be the work of their lives.

common complaints against sermons.

11. Aims of different kinds of preachers. Those who aim at strictly theological instruction. Those who take wider views.

It may be useful to take another view of the objects and aims of preaching, that in which they will present themselves when we consider them as they appear in the work of different kinds of preachers. For instance, some aim distinctly and primarily at instruction. This instruction may be of two kinds. It may be confined to theology simply, or it may embrace also history and moral science, and indeed almost all kinds of knowledge, regarding theology as a kind of *summa philosophia*, which harmonizes and gives its proper place and highest aim to all we know. Those who aim chiefly at what is generally understood by strictly theological instruction, undertake a very difficult task, for they are speaking upon what all the congregation, in its leading facts and mother-ideas, are already acquainted with, and which cannot be spoken upon well and interestingly, and so as really to instruct, without a complete knowledge of the subject and much logical acumen. What we find however to be the fact is, that very many of those who aim in their sermons at merely doctrinal instruction seldom go beyond the quotation of texts, which is a very dry way of dealing with the subjects they handle, and, as Jeremy Taylor observes, a very inconclusive way. Those who take the other and wider view of the instruction sermons may be made to convey, propose to themselves a very high aim indeed, but one which is certain to be attended with lamentable and ludicrous failures, unless the preacher be provided with very extensive learning and with very sound judgment.

12. Those who aim at awakening religious emotion.

A second description of preachers make it their object to awaken and feed religious emotion. It is obvious that very little knowledge is required for this purpose. A man who is very ignorant of books may still, if he feels those emotions himself, be able to communicate them to others. This is the aim of a large proportion of those whom we call popular preachers. These preachers are very serviceable to large classes of the community. For it has always hitherto been the case (and we may suppose that it will continue to be so), that the great majority of mankind, being engaged throughout their lives in daily business and daily toil, have been so unlearned that more could be effected by awakening their religious feelings than by endeavoring to convey to them religious instruction. But the very qualification which makes these preachers useful, the fact of their preaching being chiefly emotional, is the reason why we so rarely find them possessing much weight in the world of intellect. It is a rare thing to find those who are able to teach well, able also to move the feelings well; and so, too, *vice versà:* in the Ministry, however, of the Word there is a place for each.

13. Those who regard sermons as a department of the *Belles Lettres.*

A third class, that was very numerous in the last generation, but is now very much on the wane, make it their aim to give pleasure to critical ears by the propriety of their ideas, language, and style. They hardly regard a sermon as any thing more than a literary composition. Sermons with them are a department of the *Belles Lettres*. Bishop Porteus's sermons and a large portion of Bishop Heber's were of this kind. But nothing more need be said of this class of preachers, as the growing earnestness of religious feeling is rapidly extinguishing them.

14. Those who disparage sermons.

A fourth class aim at producing a kind of quietism—I had almost said, no effect at all—by their preaching. They find the other parts of the ritual more productive than the sermon of those emotions they themselves delight in; and some of the members of their congregations are soon brought to the same way of thinking and feeling; they therefore discountenance and disparage any kind of preaching that is accompanied with excitement, or almost with interest. We sometimes hear them even objecting to preaching altogether. It would not be correct to say that they regard the sermon from the ritualist's point of view, because the sermon is a part of the ritual; nor would it be right to say that they are altogether in the wrong, for many sermons produce what cannot be considered as a religious effect upon the minds of those who hear them: many controversial sermons, and many that are not controversial, are of this kind. The deep and calm feelings too which these preachers aim at cultivating, though not all adapted to, or attainable by the mass of mankind, are true and beautiful, and ought to be exhibited to the world, but the inert, the ignorant, and the contentedly sinful, will never be awakened by a refined quietism.

15. Those who regard sermons as a part of the service. Those who regard them as a part of their duty.

These are the different kinds of preachers who by their energy and talents are brought into prominence. There are, however, two other classes, each of which is probably more numerous than all the preceding four combined. First, those who have no definite aim in their preaching, merely regarding the sermon as a part of the service they have to perform; and, secondly, those who without any great amount of learning, or the possession of any popular talent, endeavor to set the Gospel before the souls which have been entrusted to their spiritual oversight. They feel their responsibility, and endeavor to discharge their duty faithfully. It is the attention of this class, particularly of the younger portion of it, that I am desirous of obtaining for the suggestions of these pages. I wish them to consider whether it is not within their reach to make their preaching a far more effective instrument for good than they have hitherto found it, by devoting to it that amount of time, study, and labor, without which nothing very great, or very good, can be attained in any department of human exertion.

CHAPTER V.

SOME REMARKS ON THE PLACE ASSIGNED TO PREACHING IN THE WORD OF GOD, AND IN OUR SERVICE.

1. The place assigned to preaching in the Word. First in the Old Dispensation.

I NOW propose to consider the way in which the Word itself speaks of this instrument for its own propagation, exposition, enforcement and adaptation to the varying circumstances of the times. Under the Old Dispensation the prophetical office, that now held by the properly-qualified Minister of the Word, was, we may almost say, the only means used for maintaining and advancing the knowledge of God. In times as rude and unsettled as those were, the religious and moral forces of society are always likely to organize themselves for the protection of society. At such epochs this organization will stand forth more prominently than at others. It was so again in the Middle Ages. And it will also happen that whatever is done by the organization of these forces of society will seem to those who, like ourselves, regard the history from a distance, and with the aid of only very brief and imperfect records, very much as if it were the work of the leaders only. But it is obvious that, to have enabled them to carry out the bold and difficult tasks in which we frequently find them engaged, the sympathy and support of considerable numbers were requisite. And as respects their teaching, it must be equally obvious that unless the truths and sentiments they enunciated had been previously more or less distinctly apprehended by others, what they might have said would have fallen to the ground. The position therefore in which the Hebrew prophet stood towards his own times, was not that of complete difference from, or opposition to the religious thought and feeling of those around him, but that he saw more clearly, and was able to enunciate more forcibly than others what was at work in many minds besides his own. The Spirit of God, which guides to a knowledge of the truth, and supplies the boldness to say and to do what is required for its maintenance, was in him in greater measure than in others. Because he saw distinctly truths which others had seen, but seen less distinctly, or perhaps which others were only prepared to see, he became to them the messenger of God to proclaim these truths to them. Had it been otherwise, what he enounced would have fared as good seed fares when it falls upon dry and naked rock. Be this, however, as it may, just what we are told of David, as a prophet, that "the Holy Ghost spake by his mouth," the father of the Baptist declares was true of "all the prophets which had been since the world began." They were raised up in long succession, through God's providence, to proclaim by preaching each advance to a purer and higher morality, and to a more spiritual religion, and to awaken and keep alive the assurance of the ultimate triumph of good over evil, of right, of mercy, and of truth. Each progressive revelation of God's Holy Spirit, and every application of previously secured truths and principles to the wants of the times, was made through this instrumentality. We have no intimation of any other way in which these things were or could have been done.

2. Then in the New. But to pass from the old Dispensation to the New. Here it is that we behold the prophetical office exalted to its highest dignity, and exercised on the widest scale. The Son of Man has now taken that office on Himself. The Word has become flesh, and is shining as the Light of the world; and preaching, we find, is the only instrument He uses for disseminating the Light. The preacher and the prophet in Him are synonymous. "He went through every village and city preaching the glad tidings of the kingdom of God." All His parables, and discourses, and teaching of every kind, were delivered as spoken words, that is to say, were preached. It had been in this way that he who was "the prophet

of the Highest" had prepared the way for Him: "In those days came John the Baptist preaching." And after a time we find the Great Preacher sending forth the twelve to preach the kingdom of God. And then He appoints other seventy also, and sends them two and two before His face into every city and place whither He Himself would come, to preach. The miracles He empowered them to do were to support their preaching. And after the Ascension of their Divine Instructor, His disciples go forth to preach His Gospel in all the world, as they had been commanded; miracles again being made subsidiary to preaching; for "they went forth and preached every where, the Lord working with them, and confirming the word with signs following." The object of the great miracle on the day of Pentecost, as described in anticipation by the Lord Himself; and as shown by the nature of the powers it conferred, for it gave knowledge and words; and as seen by its effects; was to enable those who were acted on by it to preach: and so it happened, not accidentally, that the first propagation of the Gospel was the direct and immediate result of preaching. And this was the instrument, as I have already had occasion to notice, by which Paul and his brother-Apostles established the Gospel in the world. "God," he says, "was pleased by the foolishness of preaching to save them that believe." Again he says, in writing to Titus, "God in due time manifested His Word through preaching." And in speaking of himself to Timothy he says not only that he had been appointed "an Apostle and a teacher of the Gentiles," but also, and he puts it first, as being foremost in his thoughts, "a preacher" of the Gospel, though indeed each of the three titles to a great extent implies the other two. In his Epistle to the Romans he greatly magnifies and insists on the necessity of the office: "How shall they call on Him on whom they have not believed? and how shall they believe on Him of whom they have not heard? and how shall they hear without a preacher?" supporting what he says by a reference to the prophet Isaiah: "How beautiful are the feet of those who preach the Gospel of peace, and bring the glad tidings of good things!" So was the Gospel established in the world by preaching. And by this same means was it, as I have shown elsewhere, maintained and extended. And whenever the love men had for it was languishing and dying away, this was the instrument used for its revival. Every Minister of the Word should consider the exhortation which the great preacher Paul urged upon his brother-preacher Timothy: I charge thee therefore before God and the Lord Jesus Christ, who will judge the quick and dead at His appearing in His kingdom; preach the Word; be instant in season and out of season;

reprove, rebuke, exhort with all long-suffering and doctrine.

Such is the way in which preaching is set before us in the Word of God.

3. Preacher, how far synonymous with prophet.

In the preceding paragraphs I have been using the words Preacher and Prophet, and Preaching and Prophesying, as nearly synonymous. And so for our present purpose they may be regarded. The prophets were preachers of the Word of the Lord; God spake by their mouths. In this sense the Apostles were prophets, and Jesus Christ is the Head of the prophetic order. And so in His Church every preacher who speaks in conformity to the will of God, and who advances, or even maintains among men the knowledge of God, which includes the duty of man, belongs to the same order as the prophets of old. "For the prophecy came not in old time by the will of man; but holy men of God spake as they were moved by the Holy Ghost."

4. The want of preachers still, and always will be, great.

The remark is obvious, that probably the proportion of the community that is able to read is greater now than it was in the days when the Apostle to the Gentiles went forth to preach the Gospel to the nations on the northern shores of the Mediterranean. But no great weight need be attached to this remark, although we add to it that the facilities for reading have increased since the Apostle's time in a still greater degree even than the proportion of readers; because amongst ourselves the absolute number of those who require the aid of the preacher is so great that we are unable to supply the want. The want is great and pressing in every part of the country. In respect of this matter we cannot talk of some towns or some neighborhoods being more enlightened than others, for the difference between the most and the least enlightened is so inconsiderable as to make scarcely any practical difference. Can we put our finger on any place, and say, "The preacher is not needed here; his labors may be transferred elsewhere?" Indeed the probability seems to be that the preacher will always be needed even by the most cultivated classes, for wherever religious feeling exists the preacher satisfies a desire which is felt by most of us. Religion has been regarded by statesmen and historians as the strongest of all bonds of union. And so it is; it binds nations, and races, and sects together in a manner which nothing else can. And it has this effect because the religious sentiment, being in its highest form and expression Christian love, in whatever degree it may exist, in the same degree will it crave for sympathy, for union and communion of feeling; and for a large assembly to be consciously moved in common by the thoughts and feelings of one who preaches the Word of God with truth and power, is a profitable as well as a delightful way of satisfying this longing of the spirit.

5. Answer to the disparaging remark, that people do not go to church to hear sermons, but to pray.

With the facts and thoughts to which attention has just been directed, I would place in contrast the attempts now made so frequently to disparage Preaching. Sometimes this is done by the remark "That people come to church to pray, and not to hear sermons." The answer to this is, "That it is not true: people come to church both to pray and to hear sermons." Sometimes, however, the objection does not go further than an insinuation of an inferiority in Preaching to Praying. There is an ambiguity in this way of putting the objection, and it will be almost an answer to it to state it in such a manner as to remove the ambiguity. There cannot properly be any comparison between Preaching and Praying, because they are not the acts, which the objection would require them to be, of the same person. The one is the act of the Minister, and the other the act of the congregation. The comparison then must be between the advantage of listening to sermons and the advantage of praying. The method of the argument is to affirm that the benefits of the latter greatly preponderate over the benefits of the former, and to put this statement in such a way as to insinuate that it is safe and profound to sneer at and depreciate preaching as a matter of little consequence. There is no weight at all in this argument. First, benefit is a word of relative significance. There may be some to whom, for satisfactory or for unsatisfactory reasons, that may be of little benefit which will be of much benefit to many. Far the greater part of the population of this country, some even perhaps of the educated classes, may still be in need of being taught not only how to pray aright, but to pray at all in the proper sense of the word praying. As yet, to them the benefit of the opportunity of praying, of which they cannot or do not avail themselves, is not of so much value as the opportunity of hearing sermons, which may lead them to prayer. It is also a sufficient reply to the objection to point out the fact that there are two kinds of sermons, good sermons, by which all may be benefited, and bad sermons, from which very little good can result to any one; the carelessness, ignorance, and tediousness of which really often do much harm. The objection includes both kinds, whereas it cannot apply to the former, that is to say, to what all sermons ought more or less to be.

6. And that hearing sermons is inferior to praying.

Another and somewhat similar way of attempting to depreciate preaching is to affirm that hearing sermons is inferior to praying, because preaching is a means used for bringing men to praying; and that the end must be greater than the means. The weight, however, of this objection is not greater than the weight of the one we have just disposed of. It is possible that that which is the means for attaining several great ends may, in regarding a whole system, be as important a part of that system as any one of those ends taken separately. Preaching has ever been the chief means for bringing men to a knowledge of God and of duty, and for maintaining and advancing religious culture. It cannot therefore be depreciated by the fact that in a certain sense it stands to prayer in the relation of a means to an end. This is not a complete account, it is a very partial one indeed, of what preaching is. The objector (though what has just been said is a sufficient answer) may also be taken on his own ground. Why should the fact that preaching is, among its other uses, a means to prayer, be a reason for thinking lightly of preaching, any more than the fact that preaching is a means to holiness be regarded as a reason for thinking lightly of praying? He cannot depreciate preaching in this way in favor of praying, because we have only to advance a single step, and then by parity of reason prayer itself may be depreciated. The effect, however, ought to be the very opposite; for having discovered that prayer is a means to holiness, our conclusion ought to be not to neglect prayer, but to be instant in prayer. In proportion to the greatness and importance of the end is the value of the proper means for attaining that end; and preaching, we must remember, is much more than a means for bringing men to pray.

7. A cause for these objections. The truth is that these objections, just like every thing else in the world, have a cause; and with some that cause is, that the degree of freedom and of mental stir which accompanies preaching does not suit the ecclesiastical system and aims, or the sentiments of the objectors; while with others it is incompatible with that decent conforming worldliness which in so many results from the endeavor to serve both God and Mammon. These two classes of men dislike earnest preaching. It is too much of an appeal to the heart and intellect. It is too direct a challenge to thought and inquiry. It awakens. It disturbs. It individualizes both the hearer and the preacher, by calling into activity religious consciousness and the sense of duty in each. Those worldly-minded persons whose religion consists very much in outward reverence find it disagreeable to be addressed in this way. Such preaching and the effects it produces are also at variance with the feelings of those who discharge among us the necessary, or at all events, the useful part of maintaining the importance of the Church's ritual—notwithstanding the fact that the sermon they depreciate is a part of the ritual. I am speaking of what we find is the general feeling among such persons on this subject. They care little about preaching. They seem to care more even for the mere accessories of the service, such as the splendor and decorations of the sacred building, and the excellency of the music.

There is nothing annoying or condemnatory intended by those observations, for so long as a powerful party in the Church neglect the ritual, and give too much prominency to the sermon in the service, the position such objectors take up is useful, though very liable to be carried in themselves to a faulty extreme.

8. Proper length of sermons. Bad effects of making them too long.

And here I take the opportunity for offering the suggestion that the character and structure of our Liturgy, as now used, seem to indicate the propriety of not allowing our remarks to exceed over the half-hour the general practice of the Clergy, and the general opinion of the Laity on the subject assigned to them. In the Morning Service about this space of time is occupied by the Prayers, and as much more by the reading of the Word. In the Evening Service the time occupied by each of these is somewhat less. To preach, therefore, for an hour, or three quarters of an hour, appears to be both a Psychological and a Liturgical mistake. Because even if any considerable portion of the congregation had the power of attention requisite for so long a sermon—which however they have not—still so long an effort of attention given to the sermon, would, by comparison dwarf the effect of the previous reading of the Word, and of the Prayers. Much of the effect of the Word read and of the Prayers must be obliterated by the great strain laid on the mind by a sermon of an hour's length. We ought to take care that neither the devotional, nor the instructional part of the Service should detract from the effect of the other, but that each should as far as possible aid the other; and one way of providing for this is to give to each about the same space of time. In considering the point before us we may regard the reading of the Word as participating in both the above-mentioned characters, for it both conveys instruction, and excites devotion. Another concomitant of long sermons is that somehow or other, either from the accumulating effects of the fact just noticed, or because the Preacher of long sermons appears himself to take more interest in his sermons than in the other parts of the service, or from these reasons combined, the congregation, that is, those who are brought to like the practice, and the tone of mind created by it, come to think more of the sermon than of the other parts of the service, although those other parts be Prayer and Praise, and the hearing of God's Word read. Among such congregations a want of right understanding of what is meant by Public Worship is often betrayed by such questions as, "Who are we to hear to-day" and "Who preaches at such or such a Church?" The vulgar expression of "sitting under such or such a Minister" is doubly offensive, because it implies the same state of mind on this point—the feeling not that Preaching is a great thing, but that it is the great thing; and that every other part of the service is of very subordinate interest.

9. Modern failure in making the Church attractive.

It ought to be a very leading object with us all to make the Church attractive; so attractive, if possible, as that "all people should flow to it." Of late we have seen great efforts made in different quarters with this view. One party in the Church evidently rests its main hopes on Preaching. Another party of very opposite sentiments, while to a great extent discouraging preaching, makes much of the devotional part of the service; some among them carrying this principle to so unreasonable an extreme that they appear to be thinking more even of the material accessories to devotion than of the service itself. Earnestness, however, of any kind will always be attractive to many minds, and there are truths earnestly held by each of these parties that have in themselves ever been attractive; but it cannot be said of either of them, that they have rendered the Church as attractive to the great body of the people, either among the educated or uneducated classes, as those desire who wish well to the cause of religion.

10. The fault not in human nature, which, as all history shows, has a strong instinct for united worship.

We may take it for granted that the reason of this failure is not in Christianity; nor, notwithstanding what many preachers and would-be philosophers may say, in human nature. The fault is not in the latter, because there is no sentiment of our common human nature so general as, I will not say the religious sentiment, but I will speak of a very definite manifestation of that sentiment, and which bears directly on the point now before us, I mean that particular manifestation of it which exhibits itself in the manner in which in all ages, and among all races of men, and under all forms of civilization and of religion, we find men dedicating certain places and buildings to religious services, and uniting together for the purpose of public worship. Wherever we may go over the surface of the earth, if we are among men who are able to raise such structures, we find temples thronged with worshippers drawn together by the desire of gratifying their religious sentiments. There is really no feeling or practice about which there is so striking a concurrence, so general a unanimity. It would be a mistake to suppose that our churches are a result, or a characteristic of our Christianity. There has scarcely ever been a city in the world in which the grandest, costliest, and most conspicuous structures were not dedicated to the service of religion. It has been so in every quarter of the globe. Approach any city in India, in Turkey, or in China, and that which will first attract your eye, soaring above and appearing to dominate over all the other works of men's hands, will be, just as in the case of this Christian land, the sacred buildings of the place—temples, mosques, pagodas. And when some old form of civilization has passed away, all that appears to remain of it standing before our eyes, as a visible memorial of what has been, are the massive remains of its temples. Here and there you may find the mouldering fragments of some secular building, but what you find every where, as if kept up by an invisible hand, for the purpose of witnessing to us of the religious sentiments of past generation of men, are the temples. It is so with the wonderful rock temples of India, with the massive structures raised by the myriad-handed devotion of the Egypt of the Pharaohs, with the glorious remains that still rise above the sandy wastes of the Syrian desert, the rock of Athens, and the deserted fields of Pæstum, and even with the rudely grand monuments of ancient Mexico, and of our own Stonehenge. A sentiment then which has ever and every where acted with such surprising uniformity, and produced such great results, and for the gratification of which men have always been so lavish of thought and labor, can have nothing unreal or artificial about it. It cannot be due to any accidental causes. It acts with the force of a never-failing instinct implanted in the very depths of our nature by the hand of our Creator. However false, foolish, corrupt, and corrupting, creeds may have been, this sentiment has never died out: indeed, it has scarcely ever been weakened. God never left us without this witness of Himself, and of our relation to Him. It is under the influence of this sentiment that Christian churches have been built, and that Christian congregations assemble in them. We do these things in obedience to the desire our Maker has implanted in our common human nature to meet Him unitedly, to praise Him unitedly, to supplicate Him unitedly, and unitedly to have our thoughts guided to true and lofty conceptions of Him in a place and house (in order that all these things may be felt more deeply and with less of distraction) disconnected from worldly uses, and dedicated especially to Him. This is a natural, universal, indestructible sentiment, as much so as the approval of what is right, or the affection of a parent for a child. If then our churches are neglected by any large proportion of our people, this must be done not so much from any fault in human nature, as at the cost of offering violence to a strong natural sentiment.

11. Nor in Christianity. Nor is it from any fault in Christianity That religion which, by its own intrinsic power and complete adaptation to the spiritual wants of civilized man, overthrew all the religions of Europe, and of those parts of Asia and Africa at that time in connection with Europe, cannot for a moment be considered to be deficient in the power of attracting all hearts and minds to itself.

12. Those who are repelled, say it is because what is presented to them is not so much a religion as a form.

If the fault, then, is neither in our nature nor in our religion, where is it to be looked for? What is it? In what does it consist? Where does it reside? I would rather confine myself to our own Church, but it will help us in obtaining an answer to the question before us, to observe that this loss of attractive power has spread much more widely in the Church of Rome than in any other Christian body. We may almost ask what has become of the religion of Italy, of Spain, of France, and of Germany. The Pope tells us in his recent allocution that the fault is to be found in the philosophical and political speculations of the day, and in the corruptions of human nature. And many of our own religious leaders give very similar replies. These cannot be the reasons. If they were, Christianity could never have existed in the world. The true reasons must be very different from any thing of this kind. It may be as well to hear what these people say themselves, and to see whether it agrees with what those amongst ourselves say, both of the educated and uneducated classes, who have any complaints to make upon this subject. It cannot be that they are devoid of the religious sentiment. That is impossible. It may be so with an individual here and there, but it can never be the case with classes, still less with nations. They themselves do not allege any thing of this kind. It is evident that even the infidelity of the present day is not irreligious. It is puerile and false to affirm that it is. Nor is it that men have imagined any thing that they conceive to be higher or purer than the life and teaching of Jesus Christ. They frequently affirm the contrary. What they tell us is, that religion is now taught as a theology, as a system of dry dogmas, with ecclesiastical rather than human aims; and not as a religion, that is, as certain divine principles possessing a power to elevate man's nature and to guide his feelings aright, as something possessing the power of binding men to God and to one another. They say that theology, dry dogmas, are what the Churches are fighting about; are what they see inscribed on the standards which the Churches raise, and under which they urge their members to fight; whereas, what men crave for is light, love, trustfulness; what is true, what is of good report, what is lovable; what may give strength when strength is needed, and what may give rest where rest is possible; faith in God and man; hope, justice, charity.

13. This intelligible and not unreasonable or irreligious.

This is the account which those who withdraw themselves from the Ministers and ministrations of religion give of their conduct. And can we, who are the Ministers of the Word, and who in this respect stand to our brethren in Christ's place, regard the account they give of their conduct as altogether irrational, and in every sense irreligious? Rather is there not something religious in the feelings and thoughts which they thus describe to us? Would a theology and a system of dogmas have converted the Roman Empire and established Christianity in the world? Very few, I think, would be of opinion that they could have produced such effects. And as moral no less than political empire is maintained by the same means by which it is acquired, I do not think that Christianity can be upheld by this method of preaching it and presenting it to men's minds. Does the artisan class, the one amongst us which has broken to the greatest extent with the Church, do the men of science, and do the wretched in any way (and in these days the forms of mental as well as of other kinds of distress are very numerous), feel that what they are in need of is a theology and dogmas? When therefore we offer these to them in the first place as spiritual food and light, we can understand what they say when they tell us that they are repelled; that they felt that they were asking for the bread of life, and we offered them a stone,—something very cold and hard.

14. Christianity, as presented by Jesus Christ and the Apostle to the Gentiles had power to convert the world.

What then are we to do? Are we to give up our theology and our dogmatic teaching? If we were to do this, we could hardly be regarded any more as a Church. But what we must do, if it can be done, is to find out what men really want, and to supply their wants, remembering that the Gospel when first preached to the world exactly met the wants of those spiritually distressed times. The fact that the world accepted Christianity without the application, in spite even of the use on the other side, of force, voluntarily, and often at great cost, proves that it supplied a deeply-felt want. It also proves that men are not irrational in this matter, and that they are not irreligious; for the very thing they require is, that their reason and their religious wants should be really and truly satisfied. This has been done once, and so may be done again, if attempted in the same way in which it was originally done. What Christ did, and felt, and taught, and what Paul did, and felt, and taught, was what converted the world. Here then is what we who are Ministers of the Word must endeavor to do, and to feel, and to teach, setting before all that to do and to feel in this way will be emancipation and happiness.

15. The satisfying plenteousness of God's house, as apprehended by the Psalmist.

If we could rekindle the feeling described in the thirty-sixth Psalm, we might then be sure that our work was being well done; if making the Church attractive can be regarded as a proof of our doing our work well. "The children of men shall be satisfied with the plenteousness of Thy house; and Thou shalt give them to drink of Thy pleasures as out of a river. For with Thee is the well of life, and in thy light shall we see light." God is the well of life, and God is the light that we desire; and in the act of united worship in His house, may not men attain to large measures of that light and that life, and so become satisfied with the plenteousness of His house?

16. The excellence of our form of public worship, as compared with those services which make too much of preaching.

Our own form of public worship appears to supply us with every thing that is requisite for this purpose. In this respect it is quite unequalled. We must regard it as aiming at satisfying the wants both of the heart and of the understanding; for religion is the offspring not of one of these only, but of both, that is of our whole moral nature; and regarding our Liturgy in this way, we shall find, I think, that it provides with more than human wisdom and insight for every thing that a religious service or public worship can require. Some Christian bodies err in maintaining services which aim almost exclusively at imparting instruction. This is evident from the fact that with them the sermon is the main feature of the service. Every thing else is subordinated to it. This is a very serious mistake, because it is a misconception of the main object of a religious service. It sends away those who should have been worshippers without their having had presented to them any proper opportunity for worship. Many of the religious emotions which belong to worship have by such services not been gratified, or even awakened.

No food is provided for them: they are starved. Services of this kind have a chilling and hardening effect. They minister to a spirit of controversy, and to arrogancy.

17. And with those which disparage it.

It is possible, as we all know, for a Church to err in the opposite direction. It may attach so little importance to the sermon, or may have a repugnance to the liberty of prophesying, as in most of its services to dispense entirely with the exposition of the Word of God. This is to depreciate the Word of God, or to be afraid of it. The main, almost the whole, effort that is made, is to awaken religious emotion, to sway the heart. Every means has been resorted to for bringing this about; incense, vestments, pomp, processions, ceremonies, symbolisms, music, painting, sculpture, architecture. Every thing that has power to stir emotion, as distinct from thought, has been attended to. The understanding alone is not appealed to, just as if there were something to be dreaded, or even something unholy in the understanding; or as if, at all events, it had nothing to do with religion. It is well that the religious emotions should be cultivated, but ill that this should be done without the aid of the understanding; the consequences of which we see are indistinctness and ignorance in matters of religion, that is to say, the substitution of superstition for religion.

18. How the different factors of a religious service are balanced in our Liturgy.

Our admirable Liturgy avoids what is faulty in these two extremes, and combines what is good in each. It neither allows the exposition of the Word of God to reduce the rest of the service to insignificance, nor does it regard it as a matter of small account. Just so too with the devotional part of the service. It does not allow that to overpower the instructional part, or to be overpowered by it. Each is duly considered and adequately provided for. The provision made for religious instruction is, that the whole of the Word of God should be read through in the course of the year, the Psalms twelve times, and the New Testament, with the exception of the Book of the Revelation of St. John, three times, with the addition of certain portions of the Gospels and Epistles being selected for a fourth repetition; and that, furthermore, on every occasion of public service, a part, or some point of God's Word should be expounded. The provision made for pure devotion supplies means and opportunities for the expression of every kind of religious emotion,—confession, humiliation, supplication, the making known our wants to God, the thanking and praising Him for all His goodness, the sense of pardon, reconciliation, and acceptance. Nothing that can call forth religious emotion, or to which religious emotion can desire to give utterance, has been omitted.

19. The effect of this admirable service may be weakened through faults in those who conduct it.

We may then, I think, infer, that wherever so admirable a service fails to draw men to the house of God, having become incapable of satisfying the natural instinct for united public worship, there must be something elsewhere than in the service itself very wrong. Whatever circumstances of the day there may be that bear upon and affect the conclusions and feelings of certain classes among us, I pass by, because their direct consideration does not belong to my subject. There may, of course, be faults in certain individuals and in certain classes, and some of the circumstances of the times may be adverse to a right appreciation of our service; but there may also be faults in the Minister who conducts the service. This last particular is all that my subject now requires me to advert to. He may be wanting in devotion, or in learning, or in some qualification needed for enabling him to conduct the service in such a manner as shall satisfy the religious feelings of the congregation.

20. The high and responsible duty of the Minister of the Word in this matter.

The foregoing pages aim at indicating what in some cases may be the remedy when the cause of the failure is in the Minister. The service, even if absolutely perfect in itself, cannot do every thing. Much will still depend on the way in which it is conducted, that is, on the Minister. In this, after all, lies his chief duty as a Minister of the Word. Those committed to his charge are assembled before him. He is leading their intercourse with God. He is delivering to them God's Word, and speaking to them all, collected for this purpose, of the things belonging to their salvation. If it is important that he should be able to speak to them individually on this subject, as occasions present themselves, how much more important is it that he should be able to speak to them all collectively. Many of them he never sees at any other times. How solemn and imperative then is the duty of the Clergy to take care, by the way in which they perform their part of the service, that its effect is not weakened, and no discredit brought upon it! In this matter a heavy, a very heavy responsibility, devolves upon them. They have to take care that the instructional parts do really convey instruction, and that the devotional parts are led in such a manner as really to awaken and sustain devotion. To do these things as they ought to be done requires very high attainments, and is an offering to God worthy of the mind and of the heart He has given to man. The Minister of the Word is bound by the most sacred considerations not to aim at any thing less. The man who attains to this high aim makes a worthier contribution to the service of God, and does more to elevate its character, than he would have done had he built a cathedral of marble, decorated with gold and precious stones, for the service to be performed in; for the service is greater than the temple; and the mind and heart, to which the service gives expression, are more precious than rubies and fine gold, and all the things we can desire for ourselves or dedicate to God are not to be compared to them.

SERMONS.

THE remainder of the volume will contain notes of six sermons I preached while occupied on this work, followed by six studies for sermons. In each case the notes were written after preaching, from recollection of what had been said, aided by the few brief memoranda that had been made at the time of the study of the subject, and which were made in order that the plan and arrangement which had then been thought out might not be forgotten. The reader will readily see that the sermons are not finished compositions, such as would admit of being read from the pulpit, but merely what they profess to be, notes of what was said.

I propose to append to each sermon a few observations. These will be of two kinds; for I wish to comment both on their matter and on their structure and composition; that is to say, both on what is said, and upon the way in which it is said. Indeed, my object in giving the sermons will be contained in the observations which will follow them, for it is my wish to use them as illustrations of the rules and advice I have given in the preceding part of this work.

It may appear an unusual proceeding for a writer to comment on his own work; and so I must explain why I am about to do this. I do it because I am obliged to do it; for it would not be allowable for me to reprint half-a-dozen sermons from other people's works. I must therefore give sermons of my own. And as to commenting upon them, I shall be able to do this with much more freedom and ease when my own compositions are the subject of the comment, for I shall know why I said one thing and not another; and what is the meaning and purpose of each sermon, and of each part of each sermon.

The reader, too, when he finds that the sermons are the work of the writer who has undertaken to give him advice on the very subject of the composition of sermons, will be more disposed to make his own remarks and to form his own judgment upon them than he would be were they taken from other people's works.

I have throughout the foregoing pages insisted on the principle that the preaching of the Minister of the Word can rest only on the Word itself. And I have endeavored to make it clear that I mean by this that his preaching must exhibit not an ignorant familiarity, but what in the opinion of competent judges is well-informed and intelligent acquaintance with the Word; that is to say it must include a knowledge of all that in these days contributes to a full and right understanding of it. An address that does not show this is not an exposition of the Word of God, is not a sermon, but the speech of an ignorant man that will repel all who are not as ignorant as the speaker himself. For the Word of God is the truth on all matters of duty and religion as far as God has permitted it to be revealed to the existing generation; and the prophet, or preacher, is the man who having attained to a knowledge of this truth delivers it effectually to those who have not attained, and who indeed never will be able to attain to it, without his aid.

A sermon must also be felt to be the address of a Christian to Christians; of one who does himself feel the truth, the force, and the value of what he is setting before others. The convictions and the experiences he is speaking about are his own. He has suffered from what he describes as evil. What he commends as good and profitable he has found good and profitable to himself. The words of an exponent of Theology are one thing, and the words of a Christian Minister are quite another thing. The flavor and effect of the two are very unlike. The faculties even to which they are addressed are not the same; for the former are submitted to the critical, and the latter to the moral faculties.

One word more: all worship is communion with God. Without this communion of man's spirit with God's Spirit there can be no religion. It is therefore not only useless, but a positive and direct injury to the cause of religion that a man, whose daily life and bearing are inconsistent with the idea of habitual communion with God, should stand up before the Lord's congregation, as Jesus did in the Synagogue of Nazareth, to speak about the things of the kingdom of God. What the Preacher may have to say must be gathered from many sources, some old, some new; but every thing he says ought, and that manifestly, to have been sifted, harmonized, and sanctified by communion with God, by prayer.

SERMON I.

ISAIAH xxviii. 10.

"Here a little, and there a little."

It can result only from a narrow and mistaken view of religion to suppose that any of the conclusions of observation or experience which may contribute towards enabling us to form a correct estimate of human life, and to act wisely under the circumstances in which we are placed here, can be unimportant. It is possible that a statement may contain nothing distinctively Christian, and yet, by its truth and wisdom, may be very serviceable to one desirous of doing good Christian work.

Consider what the words "here a little, there a little," suggest. Certainly nothing religious or Christian in the ordinary acceptation of those words. They convey nothing doctrinal. Nevertheless they are full of true practical wisdom, which it would be folly to regard as something separate from religion. The idea contained in them is, that we are not to expect to be always engaged in what we may consider important undertakings, or to be always making what we may consider rapid progress. We must at times be content with work that appears to us very humble, and with progress that appears to us very slow; with only a little here, and a little there.

This is just one of the most necessary lessons for the enthusiastic, the zealous, and the half-informed. They are always looking for what they regard as great things. They are always impatient of delay. But if they would add knowledge, and wisdom, the fruit of knowledge, to their zeal, they would learn that there is "a day of small things" as well as a day of great things. Resistance of one kind or another, from one quarter or another, is always springing up to hinder our undertakings; and so seldom indeed would it be good even for a good cause to have every thing its own way, that the days of small things are to the days of great things as thousands to one. The man who is wise in knowing this, while he sets before himself what, according to the light that is in him, he conceives to be the highest and best objects, and lives for them, will not be discouraged because he finds that he can seldom do more than "a little here, and a little there."

In nature, as we are beginning to understand, all great changes are effected very gradually and very slowly. Continents are not built up, mountain ranges are not elevated, oceans are not excavated by sudden efforts. These grand operations are carried through so gradually, that the rate of progress is quite inappreciable to man, even when by the aid of letters his memory, or rather his view of the past, is enabled to reach back for three or four thousand years. These things have been done over the whole of our earth, so as to make every part of its surface what it now is; the same causes, producing similar results, are every where in operation at this moment; but the rate at which the progress has been, and is still being carried on, is inconceivably slow.

Add another remark: this slow rate of progress in nature is God's work. It comes from His mind. It is His doing. He it is who is so many thousands of years in excavating the bed of an ocean, and in constructing a continent. And the agents He employs for doing His work are either themselves so small, or must work so slowly, that any rapid progress is simply impossible. Perhaps large districts of future continents are being formed from fragments of microscopic animalcules; while the now existing continents are being worn away by the gradual erosion of rains, and rivers, and tides, and waves, and winds, and frost. In these things God does every thing very gradually, "a little here, and a little there."

Now it is probable that the Being who thinks it

best to act in this way with respect to the material world in which He has placed man, will act in a similar way with respect to man himself; man and the world in which he is placed being the correlated parts of one plan. The same mind underlies and regulates the progress of both. When we come to the facts of the case, we find that they support the supposition. The greatest event that has taken place in the history of the world was the development and establishment of our religion; and how instructive is the review of the gradual way in which it was brought about! Take the particulars as they are recorded in the Holy Scriptures. Sin entered into the world when the first man transgressed. But how many thousand years elapsed before the appearance on the scene of Him who was to overcome sin, and to be our guide into the perfect way of righteousness! The steps by which God prepared the world for His coming were slow and gradual, almost beyond any thing we can imagine. The patriarchs, the chosen people, the law given through Moses, the prophets, were only a few of the later steps in the long line of events, which issued at last, when the fulness of time was come, in the state of necessary preparation. In other parts of the world other lines of events had to be carried through, and other equally necessary results matured. Millennium after millennium was required for this purpose, and was passed in this way.

Then, when all things were at last made ready, consider how gradually the actual establishment of the Gospel was brought about. It was not done by a sudden decree, or by an instantaneous exercise of omnipotence. The Saviour appeared as an infant, and grew to man's estate just like any other child of man. He then delivered the Gospel by the slow process of preaching it—a process necessarily of some years. He was then content to leave this earth without having effected its establishment. Were there half-a-dozen persons in all who understood His Gospel and believed on Him at the time when He gave up the ghost on the Cross? Certainly there were not. And so the Apostles were commissioned, and instructed by the Spirit, and sent forth to continue the preaching the Lord had commenced. In this gradual way the Gospel of man's redemption was begun to be spread and established in the world. The rule observed was that of working gradually, "a little here, and a little there."

Nearly two thousand years have passed since that time; and in what way and at what rate has the Gospel been advancing over the world? Only very gradually. Many countries it has not yet reached. In some it has receded. This is one of those eras in which visible progress is being made; but still it is not being made in the way in which zeal would have anticipated, but through events which it took who can tell how many thousands of years to arrive at? The chief cause of its present spread is, that at length, through the progress of science, and from political and economical causes, some of the nations that have received Christianity, and above all others our own countrymen, are now able to penetrate to and establish themselves in the wide waste places of the earth.

I have still to show what practical bearing these remarks have upon ourselves, upon our thoughts, our feelings, and our conduct. The lesson which stands out upon the surface of what we have been considering is, that what we are called to is to work, and still to work on, and to faint not. And we must not judge of the value of our work by the success which has attended it, or by the rapidity of its progress. The questions we must ask ourselves are such as whether our work is precious in the sight of God, who judges not as men judge, by immediate, tangible, ponderable results? And are its effects good upon our own characters? These are quite distinct questions from what is the amount of effect it has had upon others and upon the world. We are too much disposed, in forming our estimates, only to regard the latter consideration. This is a mistaken and unfortunate way of judging. If the Omnipotent and All-wise is content to work slowly, why should we be impatient? The motto of him who in this respect has learnt of God, and who has in himself the mind that was in

Christ Jesus our Lord, will be, Rest not, Haste not. Trust in God.

I say that one way of estimating our work is to consider in what way God will estimate it. Remember, God does not require one man to do every thing, nay, not even to do much; any more than He requires one generation of men to do every thing, or even to do much. What He requires of a man is that he should do what He has set him to do, and what He has set him to do is that he should with all his heart do and bear whatever it is evident to conscience with common sense for its assessor he is called upon to do and to bear. Lazarus was called to suffering; to bless God under the deprivation of all that is pleasant to flesh and blood; and furthermore, in the midst of much that is most distressing. Here the busy philanthropist or the eager controversialist might say was a form of life in which no one particle of work could be done. How could he who was so circumstanced be useful to any one? But God does not think in this way, otherwise He would at once ordain that there should be no more Lazaruses upon earth. Nay, rather looking upon this poor sufferer as occupying a place in a great plan ordained by God, we must come to the conclusion that his life was one of great usefulness, issuing in great reward. Considered in this light we can understand that his abject condition, his penury of every thing that makes life desirable to the multitude, his having none but God to help him, his pain-racked, corruption-eaten body, were to a large portion of the inhabitants of a self-willed, and self-seeking capital, a very intelligible call to think of God and of a day to come; a call to feel for the distressed; and, as stewards of God's bounties for this very purpose, to succor them; a call to consider the conditions God has imposed on human life, as for instance the frail tenure by which they themselves held their good things, their health, their wealth, and all their temporal advantages. Who could tell how soon he might not himself be made in some respect or other no better than this poor beggar? The daily sight of so abject a sufferer possibly was a more effectual sermon to the inhabitants of Jerusalem than all the preaching of all who then sat in Moses' seat. He who could do nothing may have done more, without opening his mouth, than they all with all their learning, position, and influence. And we are told how highly God estimated his work, for He took him to Himself. If a man is honest and enduring, if he is resigned and self-denying, if he is pure and true, is he not doing God's work? And is not the light that shines from him that which God approves? Is this work that God will think lightly of? We must bring this home to ourselves. What is required of us is not great results as men count greatness; if it were, few men would ever have done God's work in the world.

Rather let us feel that there never lived a man who loved and trusted God, who believed in His justness and goodness, who walked as in His presence, but did His work abundantly and acceptably.

I just now mentioned another way of estimating our work—that of considering the effect it has upon our own character. We are told that there are men who will say at the judgment, "Lord, Lord, have we not cast out devils in Thy name? and in Thy name done many marvellous things?" to whom the Lord will say, "Depart from me, for I never knew you, ye workers of iniquity." These were they who were called to great position and opportunities, who had power, wealth, authority, influence, learning, culture, intellectual capacity; and who, merely because it was their place to do it, did something, a thousand-fold be it, more than the humbly placed could appear to do; but the love of what is good and true and gentle, that is the love of God, the one source of all excellence, was not in them; and so what they did had no good effect upon their hearts. They did not become better men, more loving, more self-denying, more patient, more gentle. Estimate then the work you have done, and are doing, in this way: not by attempting to measure its effects upon others, but by measuring its effects upon yourself. Estimated by this standard, many a man whose life-long, daily, lowly, monotonous occupation has been in the workshop or at the plough, has worked to better purpose in the eyes of the great Task-master, has become more purified, better instructed, more sanctified, brought nearer to God by his work, than some of those who in the world's estimation have occupied a high place among its benefactors.

These considerations throw some light upon those graces which are more especially Christian, enabling us to see what they are in themselves, and what they are good for. For instance, they help us to comprehend the meaning of Humility. If the opportunities, and means, and endowments God has vouchsafed to us are but small, if He allows us to do but little, and to advance in doing that little but slowly, when we have learnt of God the lesson before us to-day we shall acquiesce. We shall feel and understand that His mind is in the matter; that it is in this way that He has thought it best to deal with us. We shall be contented, thankful, hopeful, trustful. We shall not complain because He has not allowed us a wider field, or called us to greater things. Such is the spirit of Christian Humility.

Again, the facts and the thoughts that have been before us show how necessary a part of the Christian character is Perseverance, that patient continuance in well-doing of which we read. We must not be discouraged at finding that we have nothing of importance to do as the world measures importance; or that our efforts have been attended with little success, as the world understands success. Our business is to persevere unto the end: the rest belongs to God.

With Faith also the connection of all this is very close, and well worthy of notice. It is of the essence of Faith to trust God in all that He does, and under all circumstances. As soon as we shall have learnt that slow progress in every thing good is a law God has imposed upon the course of this dispensation; that His plan here, certainly in things moral and spiritual is not to perfect any thing, but to allow of gradual advances towards perfection, for that belongs to, and will be consummated in a better world than this; then one hindrance to Faith, to childlike trustful Faith, will be at once removed. Men are not dissatisfied with what they have come to understand has been ordained of God. Failures, disappointments, repulses will not then disquiet. We shall go on, knowing that to work under these conditions belongs to this life, but that it will not always be so. We shall then travel along the paths of Christian duty, upon which God has placed us severally, assured that the man who is faithful in a little, will be accepted as though he had been faithful in much; and that he who gives the cup of cold water, if that is all his opportunities permit him to do, shall receive a disciple's reward.

Observations on the foregoing Sermon.

With respect to the foregoing sermon, I would beg permission from my younger brethren to point out to them, that its object is not merely to call attention to a truth that is of much practical value, though it is very much overlooked; but to do it in such a manner as to remind the hearers of a still more important truth, and one it is which we are only just now beginning to understand—that what our religion is depends on what our knowledge is.

It has no bearing on this statement to reply that among ourselves the ignorant classes are as susceptible of deep religious impressions as the most instructed, because those classes must always accept the religion of the age in which they live, whatever it may be. They must accept it because they have no knowledge, and cannot acquire any. The religion of the age, however, will be what the knowledge of the age makes it.

The idea of this discourse is to make the knowledge of a few simple facts belonging to the domain of one of the physical sciences, and a few analogous facts of Christian history, a ground for the cultivation of certain Christian graces. How melancholy a reflection is it that there are many amongst us who would look upon a Christian exhortation founded on such grounds as incongruous, and more likely to hinder than to advance the cause of religion. Let us consider what this implies. It shows that they regard religious truth as incompatible with scientific and historical truth; though scientific truth is simply the apprehension of the ideas which were in the mind of God before He embodied them in nature, and which ideas, at the time He set nature before us, He gave us the capacity and the desire to master; and though historical truth is simply the ascertaining the events, with their sequence and connection, which God foreordained and brought about in human affairs. Is it conceivable that the knowledge of either of these should in any way be opposed to religion? It is impossible that such knowledge can take us further from God. It must bring us nearer to Him. The more we apprehend of the principles on which God acts, so much the more of His mind will be in us. Or if any object to the repeated statements of Scripture that God's works manifest to us His mind, we may put it differently, and say—so much the more shall we form within ourselves of that mental and moral state God intended this knowledge to produce. At all events, to confine ourselves to the particulars I have mentioned in the foregoing discourse; we are told in Holy Scripture that God requires man to be humble and persevering, and to have Faith; and I think it must be plain enough that the few facts of science and history referred to in the sermon agree with Holy Scripture in commending to us these graces.

It is a distinct and especial part of the duty of the Minister of the Word, as compared with other teachers, to set forth the connection and correlation of all knowledge. Hitherto religious teachers, whether lay or clerical, have too generally assumed that their duty was directly the opposite of this. It seems to have been a main object with them to make it appear that religious knowledge is irreconcilably hostile to other kinds of knowledge, and they to it. How false and mischievous is this position!

The students of any department of human history, or of any of the natural sciences, are students of special branches. They carry on their inquiries within certain restricted and defined limits. But Divinity is truly, and essentially, and alone, the *scientia scientiarum.* If it is not this, it is nothing at all. Its subject-matter is all knowledge. The factors of the religious ideas of any age are all that is known at that time of nature and of man; that is, what is known of the ways in which God has manifested Himself in nature, and of the ways in which He has constituted and dealt with ourselves, which includes our moral being, our past history, and our present condition. The most important source of this latter department of knowledge is the Holy Scriptures.

But they are very far indeed from containing or professing to contain all that it is necessary we should know about ourselves.

If we look out over the world, we still find people among whom religion is only in its germ: a state of which history supplies us with other instances. This germ of religion is Fetishism; in other words, it is the religion of almost complete ignorance. The worshipper of a Fetish has no conception of man's history, of himself indeed he can scarcely form any conception as a moral being; and as to nature, all he knows of it is that certain objects have certain properties, but his knowledge does not go so far as to enable him to define what those properties really are, or to connect the properties of which he has a dim conception with the objects to which they rightly belong. And so he worships a feather, or a tooth. As knowledge widens and deepens, so does religion purify itself. There is no denying this, unless one would deny the teachings both of observation and of history. Every religion that now exists, or that we know of as ever having existed in the world, has been in strict correlation to the knowledge of those who made it their rule of life. As knowledge advances, religion advances *pari passu*. Religion is the knowledge men possess of God and of themselves used as a means for supplying them with a rule of life.

Again then: how unfortunate is the opposition in

which some endeavor to place religion to science and history. It is most unfortunate for themselves; for those they lead, or rather mislead; and for a time, but only for a time, for the cause of religion itself. As the difference between the religion of Fetishism and our own is simply a difference of knowledge, we ought to hail every accession to our knowledge, because it must purify, elevate, and strengthen our religion. The discoveries of Astronomers, Geologists, Botanists, Zoologists, and Chemists, have enlarged and rendered more impressive some of our ideas of God. So with those who extend our knowledge of the history and of the nature of man. We need not then have any dread of the extension of knowledge. If its extension be, from a religious point of view, an evil, how much have we now to dread, for it is certainly now being extended with a rapidity wholly unknown in former times. But what ground can there be for believing that we have reached, or ever shall reach a point at which the laws of mind will be so far reversed, as that knowledge which has hitherto built up shall thenceforth overthrow religion? From a date long anterior to the time of Galileo, there has existed a most pernicious misunderstanding between religion and knowledge. They have feared, hated, reviled each other. Under the Old Dispensation we see no trace of this feeling. There religion is distinctly based on knowledge. And now, again, there are symptoms of their true relation to each other being better understood. We may say this when we see many Ministers of Religion cultivating, welcoming, and disseminating knowledge; and this with a clear perception of the extent to which religion is dependent upon it; and when, on the other hand, we see men of science no longer denouncing religion, but regarding their sciences as contributory to it.

SERMON II.

WHAT WE ARE TO SEEK IN LIFE.

2 CORINTHIANS xi. 23—27.

"In labors more abundant, in stripes above measure, in prisons more frequent, in deaths oft. Of the Jews five times received I forty stripes save one. Thrice was I beaten with rods, once was I stoned, thrice I suffered shipwreck, a night and a day I have been in the deep; in journeyings often, in perils of waters, in perils of robbers, in perils by mine own countrymen, in perils by the heathen, in perils in the city, in perils in the wilderness, in perils in the sea, in perils among false brethren; in weariness and painfulness, in watchings often, in hunger and thirst, in fastings often, in cold and nakedness."

THIS is a description of the life the Apostle Paul had been passing for several years. It was a life of ceaseless toil, peril, suffering, unjust treatment, and insult. Many must be struck with the thought that he who had to bear all this must have been a very wretched man. Indeed, all who might regard the Apostle's manner of life from the ordinary point of view, that is, from the point of view from which most of us regard our own lives, would have abundant reason for coming to such a conclusion. "Here," they would think, "is not one of the circumstances which render life agreeable; no leisure, no home, no display, no pleasures; and instead of these every thing which flesh and blood most shrink from. What a miserable life! What a miserable man!" I cannot, I suppose, be wrong in taking it for granted that this is the light in which many of those who are now here present regard the description just given of the Apostle's life.

There is, however, quite another way of looking at it, and quite an opposite conclusion to be arrived at respecting it. I mean the Apostle's way of looking at it, and his conclusion respecting it. Mark, the way of looking at it, and the conclusion respecting it of the man who was himself bearing it all. In mentioning his labors, dangers, and sufferings, he does not do it with the slightest thought of lamenting himself, or in any way making himself an object of pity. He does not at all say, "See what a sufferer, what an unhappy man I am." On the contrary, he speaks of these things as if he somehow or other had satisfaction in thinking of them. The expression drops from him that "he glories in them." The remembrance of them is no more accompanied with any feeling of humiliation, than with any desire to complain. And in the following chapter we find him going so far as to say that "he takes pleasure in infirmities, reproaches, necessities, persecutions, and distresses." Nor has he a thought that fear of such treatment as he had himself received would deter men from accepting the Gospel.

It may add some weight to the judgment and example of the Apostle to remember that no one could have obliged him to submit to these miseries. Had he been so minded, he might have escaped them all. He might have stayed quietly at home, and to use our way of speaking on the subject, have enjoyed life. But this was not what he preferred. With his eyes open, seeing clearly that all these miseries would be brought upon him, of his own choice, and gladly too, he went forth and incurred them all. His address to the elders of Miletum is very moving: "And now, behold, I go bound in the spirit unto Jerusalem, not knowing the things that shall befall me there: save that the Holy Ghost witnesseth in every city, saying that bonds and afflictions abide me. But none of these things move me, neither count I my life dear unto myself, so that I might finish my course with joy, and the ministry, which I have received of the Lord Jesus." He says this of himself in the year in which he gives the account of his life we have in the text. Shortly after his making this statement to the elders of Miletum of the sufferings he expected in every city, we find the disciples at Cæsarea entreating him to have some regard for his own safety, and not to go up to Jerusalem; to this entreaty he replies, "What mean ye to weep and to break my heart? for I am ready not to be bound only, but also to die for the name of the Lord Jesus."

And furthermore he had now had five-and-twenty years' experience in this kind of life. He knew the hardness and the sharpness of all these things. For so many years had they been his daily lot. But long experience had not worked in him any desire to shrink from them, or escape from them. And in this same mind he persevered until the end came, which was only a few years later. He continued to fight the good fight, not reckoning his life dear unto himself, till at length the violent and painful death he had so long foreseen was inflicted on him. "Not tribulation, or distress, or persecution, or famine, or nakedness, or peril, or the sword, could separate him from the love of God which was in Christ Jesus our Lord. Nay, in all these things he was more than a conqueror through Him that loved him."

The reciprocal exclamations which closed the scene between the Roman Governor Festus and King Agrippa on the one side, and the prisoner Paul on the other, place in the strongest light the contrast between the two aspects of the Apostle's life. The Roman Governor, taking the worldly view, considers the Apostle mad. "Paul," he exclaims, "thou art beside thyself." To his mind it was quite irrational to expose one's self to dangers and inconveniences for spiritual or speculative objects. And just so it is among ourselves. How many think and talk in the same way of similar earnestness and self-devotion. Paul's fervid wish addressed to King Agrippa rests upon just the opposite ground: "I would to God, that not only thou, but also all that hear me this day, were almost, and altogether such as I am, except these bonds." He, the poor prisoner as they thought, brought into trouble by his ridiculous hallucinations, was so satisfied with, and so happy in his own condition, that he could have no more exalted wish for them, king and governor though they were, than that they should be as he was, with the exception of his bonds. Prisoner though he was, he was in his own estimation a happier man than any governor or king. He would not have changed his life, taking the inner life with the outer, for the life of any other man. He had nothing better to wish for them than that they should be as he was.

So was it with the Apostle—him, who after the Author and Finisher of our Faith, was its great founder. But how is it in these matters with ourselves? How far are we like-minded with him? What are we seeking? What are the ideas of happiness which are shaping our lives? These are questions which men answer in most diverse ways. And probably, we should see, if we were capable of taking all things into our consideration, that it is best that it should be so. But what each has to consider for himself is, whether his own ways are wise? Whether it would be better for him to take that view of life upon which the Apostle acted, or that on which the world acts? Are ease, pomp, show, wealth, pleasure, self-indulgence, the best objects we can set before ourselves, and what we ought to be seeking? The Apostle did not think that these things constituted the happiness of this life. Or if he did, then he thought that there was something more worthy of his pursuit than the happiness of this life. He took little thought about these things how they befell. What he gave himself up to was the practice in himself, and the extension among his fellow-men, of what he had come to know was true, and right, and good for man, being the will and the truths of God; and therefore beyond measure more desirable for man than any thing else. He would do this good; and he would purchase the satisfaction of having done it, at all personal risk and sacrifice. If happiness means ease and pleasure, his life proclaims to us that it ought not to be made the end and aim of our existence. Or if we must seek happiness, it must be a happiness of a different kind, a happiness which arises from our knowing that we are living for objects out of ourselves—what I just mentioned, for right, for truth, for God; that we are seeking the kingdom of God and His righteousness, and are on God's side. These are matters into which a man ought to look. A man ought to be able to give a reason for the conclusions on which he has staked all he has, nay all he is. What else can concern him so much?

And here the practice and the instincts of the disciples of the world appear to be better than what they avow as their principles. They talk as if ease and pleasure were happiness, and as if they were what men ought to seek. But are their lives always consistent with these ideas? Do we not see multitudes of worldly persons, I mean persons who clearly are not under the influence of religion, in their practice quite abandoning all this talk about ease and pleasure and happiness? Do we not see them taking most laboriously some to one pursuit and some to another? This is one of those points in which the children of this world are in their generation wiser than the children of light. One will devote all his powers to the attempt to advance in some branch of knowledge, or to perfect himself in some branch of art. Another will rise early, and late take rest, and eat the bread of carefulness, that he may die a rich man. Another will pass laborious days and sleepless nights, that he may stand high in reputation among men. Now these persons, though professing to believe in the world, and to have little religion, have thrown to the winds all that the world says about ease and pleasure, and are striving for their particular objects, though not in the same spirit, yet quite as devotedly as the Apostle strove for his. When then I see multitudes of the disciples of the world agreeing with the true disciples of the heavenly wisdom in devoting themselves, without regarding labors and inconveniences, to their several objects of pursuit, I must come to the conclusion that God has so made men as that they shall not be satisfied with ease and pleasure; that whether they be worldly or religious, they shall see plainly, almost, I may say, in proportion to the intelligence God has given them, that such a kind of life is low and contemptible, and that self-devotion to some pursuit is far more desirable.

There are probably not many who deliberately give themselves up to ease and pleasure; and of those who do, but a very small proportion appear to be satisfied with themselves; that is to say, are at peace with their own consciences. How frequently do we see such men restless and discontented. Their ease and pleasure do not appear so much like ease and pleasure as like uneasiness and unhappiness.

I should feel no hesitation in leaving the decision of this question to any audience, and least of all to one composed of those whom circumstances oblige to pass a life of toil and drudgery. But let us put it to ourselves. Which of the two lives is most in accordance with the faculties and purposes of our nature; the life of the Apostle who took pleasure in reproaches, in necessities, in persecutions, and distresses for Christ's sake and the Gospel's sake, or his who said, "Soul, thou hast much goods laid up for many years. Eat, drink, and take thine ease?" You feel that the Apostle respects himself and his work, and is to be honored, loved, imitated, while the other man respects nothing, and is simply contemptible. If the choice were offered to you, I think you would say, let me be the Apostle, with all his infirmities, reproaches, necessities, persecutions, and distresses, and not the poor wretch whose aspirations could not get beyond eating and drinking and taking his ease.

It seems then to come up from the very depths of man's heart and mind, the thought having been implanted in him by his Creator, that it is not good for him to have his portion in this life; that he is not here for ease and pleasure. We ought then to take counsel of this instinctive sentiment, and to consider how we can live conformably to it. It would be very serviceable to bring this distinctly before our thoughts, and, if possible, to obtain our assent to it as regards ourselves. Let us therefore put it to ourselves, each to himself: "I am not here to take my ease and pleasure, but to follow what is true and right; to do whatever God calls me to do, and to bear whatever He lays upon me." Let us say this to ourselves, and see whether we are dismayed at what it means. Let us consider whether we accept or reject it; whether it sounds to us proper and reasonable, or otherwise.

But how shall we carry out in action these sentiments? We have the account of the way in which the Apostle Paul and his fellow-Apostles, and of the way in which the Author and Finisher of our faith acted upon them. Enough was said in the first part of my discourse about the Apostle. Now look at the man Christ Jesus, in whom dwelt the fulness of the Godhead bodily. Even He pleased not Himself, but was made perfect by suffering, by labors, by self-denial—by what we call working. For the joy that was set before Him, the joy of revealing and of propagating the truth, and of doing good, He endured the Cross, despising the shame. In this way it was that He widened and relaid the foundations of the regeneration of the world. Consider how He labored and how He suffered; and remember that His sufferings came upon Him as a part of the work He had undertaken. And with respect to those sufferings, we are sure that sorrow was not the only feeling with which He was acquainted. We know that he thanked His Father in heaven at the view of the work in which He was engaged. And it cannot but have been, that in His holy and self-devoted life, the joy of which the Apostle speaks, was deeper and more soul-sustaining than was ever felt by any other of all who have been on earth in human form.

You see then, brethren, the vocation to which we are called. We must go and do likewise. God gives the opportunities and the powers for doing so. We must put God, and the truth, and goodness before every thing. One good, holy, right, and godlike action, however much self-denial it may need, and in this world of sin, such actions will always imply self-denial, one such action is worth more than whole ages of ease and pleasure. We cannot imagine ourselves having been endowed with our moral and intellectual faculties, having been enabled to carry our thoughts beyond the limits of this world, and to acquaint ourselves with God, merely that we might labor and rest, eat and drink, grow and decay, and die. The ideas are incongruous. No; the kind of actions and the kind of life I have been setting before you are far better and more desirable than any thing self-indulgence can dream of. Am I, then, rich or poor? Young or old? A child or a parent? A husband or a wife? A master or a servant? One exercising authority or one subject to it? Am I a neighbor to others? Am I a Christian? Each of these relations indicates much that I am called to do; and which I may find a satisfaction in doing hardly of this earth, because it is a satisfaction such as the world can neither give nor take away. Each of these relations is proof enough that ease and pleasure are not my first aim here; for each of them implies that there is something for me to do, the obligation to do which I cannot get rid of, because it inheres to the relation, and has upon me, as long as the relation exists, prior claims to any thing else.

Observations on the foregoing Sermon.

I have two observations to make on this sermon. The first is, that it supplies an instance of a difficulty which often, as in this case, becomes a fault in the composition of sermons. It is the difficulty of avoiding the unpardonable offence of dulness in the statement of such an argument as that set forth in the first part of the discourse before us. The object of the argument is, by calling attention to several particulars of St. Paul's life in succession, to accumulate their whole weight in favor of that view of life which supposes that there is something better worth seeking than ease and self-indulgence. In order that this effect may be produced, it is necessary to dwell for a few moments on each of these particulars. This is necessary; but the impression it produces on the mind of the hearers is bad. The impression left is: this is all very true, but it does not matter much to me. In fact, there is nothing in it to interest the thought, or awaken the feelings of ordinary hearers.

Now this difficulty may be met in two ways. First, by delivery. In society it is not uncommon to find persons who have an admirable style of talking. Their opinions are not wiser or truer than the opinions of multitudes of other men, but they are very much better put. Every thing is worded so neatly and clearly, and said in so gentle and yet so decided a manner, and in such pleasing tones, that one is never inattentive. This is not rare among conversers, but it is rare among speakers. A speaker, however, of this kind might deliver himself of a statement as dull as the one before us without its dulness being observed. He has the power of commanding attention.

The other way in which such a statement may be deprived of its dulness would be by presenting every particular of it picturesquely. This would be done by going into details, by strong coloring, and generally by calling in the aid of the imagination. This is the unvarying practice of many preachers whose names are well known. It is, however, the last method a man of good taste and good judgment would have recourse to. Such statements ought to be made with precision of thought and in quiet language; if therefore they are decked out with the flowers of rhetoric, then wrong emphasis of particulars, disproportion, and exaggeration must result.

In this case the speaker is not preaching or arguing, but is merely delivering himself of so much decorated rhodomontade. This is what cannot be done by a Minister of the Word who respects his subject, his hearers, or himself.

What then is to be done? Each must decide for himself, whether he will risk wearying his audience by such statements, or whether he will compress them into half-a-dozen lines, or drop them altogether, and set before his hearers the point under discussion only in the light of their own experience, or in some such way as will bring them to take a personal interest in it.

The other observation I have to make upon the foregoing sermon is, that it calls our attention to the very important question of how the Gospel is to be preached with reference to those circumstances of the present day which are the reverse of the circumstances of the times when it was first preached by Jesus Christ and His Apostles. It is impossible to shut our ears to the tone which the New Testament emits. The gloomiest view is taken of human life. Nor was it possible that it could have been otherwise. Consider for how many centuries, with how short intervals, the unhappy people to whom it was addressed had been trodden under foot of the heathen, Syrians, Assyrians, Egyptians, Persians, Greeks, and Romans. It is almost impossible for persons living in these times to form an adequate conception of the wretchedness, the mental and moral degradation that this had made the normal condition of the people. Probably no people except the Jews could have possessed sufficient vitality to have survived it. And it is very possible that the schooling of these long grievous centuries may have given to the race the power which it has since shown of bearing up under oppression. We may suppose, that for generation after generation those who had not this power would have a tendency to die out; and so this power might become a characteristic of the race. We can understand what so great and so long-continued suffering must have made the traditions of the time when the Gospel was first preached. And the facts of the times were in keeping with the traditions: suffering, degradation, sadness every where, and no prospect of any improvement. There was no gleam of hope in any direction. The iron had entered into their souls. Who could ever hope to see the world-wide, the omnipresent, and almighty despotism of Rome broken from off their necks? They dreamt of a deliverer, but hardly believed in one. And when Jesus came (Himself a man of sorrows and acquainted with grief), He could hold out no hope of any relief from this dreadful lot. They must go on suffering; and even worse things were in store for them. In the world they must have tribulation. This must continue, and the climax of wretchedness would be reached in the indescribable horrors that would attend the destruction of their holy city. And then would begin the endless and numberless miseries of the state in which they would neither have a place nor nation. This will quite explain the sadness that pervaded the first preaching of the Gospel, and which has been expressed by saying that it is the religion of sorrow and of the sorrowful.

The conditions of life however amongst ourselves at the present day are, in the respects I have been referring to, the very reverse of what they were in those times amongst the Jewish people. Every Englishman has for many generations and centuries stood with an unabashed face before the world and towards his fellow-countrymen. Our material prosperity is such as the world has never before witnessed. All the causes of distress that pressed upon the Jew and bore him down to the ground have been removed from us. They are unknown amongst us, and in their stead we have, in overflowing abundance, all that in these respects the heart of man can desire.

The question then arises, is that Christianity which was addressed to a suffering and unhappy world applicable, and if so how, to a world that is steeped in prosperity and happiness? When patience, and resignation, and submission are preached to us, it almost produces the feeling that we are in a position where these graces are not needed in the sense in which they were needed by those who heard the words of Christ and His Apostles. Thankfulness, moderation, and a right use of opportunities appear the more appropriate topics for exhortation to us. And this, I think, makes us feel the importance of the subject of the foregoing sermon, that is, of the example of the Apostle. If the people who occupy our streets of palaces and our country houses are not called to suffer as the Apostle and his countrymen were, they are assuredly called by the very circumstances in which God has placed them to work as the Apostle did. And they can work under far more easy and encouraging circumstances. There is a wide field every where open before them. By working, I mean honestly endeavoring at the sacrifice of personal ease, and at pecuniary cost, according to their opportunities and abilities, to do good. And what happiness can be greater than that the man is entitled to who knows that he has made others wiser, or better, or happier than they would have been without him; and who feels, as he is leaving the world, that it is in these respects his debtor?

SERMON III.

THE RETURN OF THE UNCLEAN SPIRIT.

LUKE xi. 24–26.

"When the unclean spirit is gone out of a man, he walketh through dry places, seeking rest; and finding none, he saith, I will return unto my house whence I came out. And when he cometh, he findeth it swept and garnished. Then goeth he, and taketh to him seven other spirits more wicked than himself; and they enter in and dwell there: and the last state of that man is worse than the first."

SEVERAL of our Lord's parables, as for instance those of the laborers hired at different hours, and of the man who built a vineyard and let it out to husbandmen, have very evidently two applications: one to a particular passage in the history of the Jewish nation; the other to individuals in all ages. So it is with the parable before us. Its primary application is to the chosen people. At the preaching of the Baptist and of Jesus they were much moved. They showed some desire for a closer walk with God. But they eventually fell back into a worse state than they had ever been before; for they rejected and crucified Jesus.

This makes clear what its meaning is when it is addressed to the cases of individuals. It presents to us a series of pictures in the progress of the man who dies in his sins. In the first we behold him as a man possessed with an unclean spirit. This picture intimates nothing of the earlier stages of his course. We are told nothing of the steps which brought him to this state. Neither are we told any thing of the form and character of the wickedness with which he is possessed. The forms of wickedness are infinitely various. The particular feature of sin that is indicated in the picture, and which is true of all kinds of sin, is that it is working in the man like madness. The madman is the victim of a will which is not the offspring of reason, but is opposed to reason; and which is not in conformity to, but opposed to self-interest. And yet it so masters the man that he makes no effort to resist it. If the voice of reason could command, it would be against sin. If the heart that has had experience of the miseries of sin could choose, it too would be against sin. But in the habitual sinner both the reason and the heart are in bondage. The unclean, the mad, the senseless spirit has got possession of them and rules over them. It urges the man on to his detriment, to his misery, to his ruin. You cannot in any other way account for his actions. He is possessed. He is not in his right mind.

And now we pass to the next picture. There are cases in which the cloud does not rest uninterruptedly on the mind of the lunatic. It is drifted away for a season: there is again an interval of light. Just so is it with the sinner. Something occurs that for a time shakes and appears to overthrow the power of his tyrant sin. God in his inexhaustible mercy is ever bringing this about in many ways. He recalls to the thoughts and feelings of the sinner the impressions and lessons he received in early youth from a wise and good father, or from an affectionate and religious mother. Or He overtakes him with some deserved chastisement: or He surprises him with some undeserved mercy; or He brings it about that he should witness some appalling occurrence. God is ever working by some dispensation or other on the heart and the mind of the sinner; and with apparent success in the case before us. The unclean spirit has gone out of the man. He endeavors to walk before God in his right mind. Was he profligate or a drunkard? He loathes his former profligate and drunken companions. Was he a Sabbath-breaker? He now has delight in being on God's day in God's house. Was he revengeful and malicious? He now has a pleasure in seeking to be at peace with those whom he had formerly hated. Was he unfair and dishonest? He is now endeavoring to make restitution to those he had wronged. The misleading irrational will has been overcome within him. The sight is full of promise.

But as we look on the picture that follows, the hope that had been formed within us is shaken. We behold the unclean spirit that had gone out of the man, which we had looked to see transformed into a right spirit, and able to lead the man on to a good and peaceful life, leading him "through dry places;" so that though rest is sought, none is found.[1] This incident is described with local propriety. In that hot and dry climate there can be no coolness, no refreshing air unless water be present. These things can only be found in the valley, by the streamlet's side. There the turf is green, the flowers sweet and

[1] It is obvious to remark that we do not express ourselves on this subject in the fashion of the parable, which of course was the fashion of expression used by those to whom the parable was addressed. They regarded "the unclean spirit" as having a separate existence from that of the man. It comes and goes at its own will. It returns eventually, because it is dissatisfied with the separation; and the man becomes its helpless and unresisting victim. With us "the unclean spirit" is a condition of the man's own spirit. He has powers within his reach sufficient for altering this spirit. According therefore to our form of expression, it is the man himself who expels the unclean spirit, and who, having done so, wanders through dry places seeking rest and finding none; and eventually relapses into his former state.

gay; the trees give shade; the air revives. But the half-recovered lunatic wanders in dry places, and therefore cannot but miss the cool refreshment, and the rest he is in search of. He is still exposed to the distressing glare, and the withering heat.

It often happens that the sinner who is beginning to fight against sin places himself in similar circumstances. He is entering on the most difficult work that can be undertaken by man in this world. The stream of his life having for many years flowed on in a wrong direction, he is now endeavoring to make it flow in an opposite course. He has to change the Ethiopian's skin, and the leopard's spots. The war in his mind has commenced. The good of his nature that had been subdued, has now risen up against the evil that had subdued it. But the strong man within, well equipped and armed, is holding his ground at many points. If then the would-be soldier of Christ is to come off victorious, he must be brave, and persevering, and wise.

Some there are who think the grace of God is to do every thing, and to do it in a moment. No such thing. If God's almighty power were all His nature He might do so. But having other attributes He does not do so. He looks on, and beholds the conflict. He approves, and is a fellow-worker with the man. But the man must do much himself. And one thing that he must do is that he must act wisely; and he will be doing very unwisely, for he will be bringing discouragement on himself, if he seeks for rest "in dry places."

Perhaps he has no conception of any feeling towards God excepting that of fear. He never rises to the idea that God is his Father in heaven, and that he is God's child. He does not see that God is love, and that what he is called to is himself to love. If a man see this, though he may not have attained to it, he will be encouraged by the knowledge of it. He will feel that this high state is open to him. But those whose conceptions do not go beyond fear, are in "a dry place," where they can find no rest for their souls.

Or he may be devoting himself to worldly pursuits or worldly enjoyments. I know that neither the pursuits nor the enjoyments of this world are absolutely and in themselves wrong. What is wrong is to devote one's self to them, to give them the best of our thoughts and of our affections; whereas there are higher things, the things of the soul, and of God, things whereby others may be benefited and ourselves lifted into a higher region of thought and feeling, which ought to be sought first. To invert the comparative value of the two, to put first what ought to be second, is again to seek rest in "a dry place," where it cannot be found.

But the driest of all dry places in which to seek

it, is the retention of some sin. An unclean spirit is cast out in order to pacify the conscience, and to obtain peace from God. But it is impossible that these objects can be attained if a place in the heart be still allowed to another unclean spirit. And yet we see this being done every day. Violence of temper, or an uncharitable way of thinking of others, or arrogance, or covetousness, or envy, is retained while something else is given up. How unmerciful would God be, if He allowed these persons to find rest unto their souls!

The picture again changes; but we were almost prepared for what we now behold. He—the parable says the unclean spirit, but it will be more intelligible for us to say the man—returns to his house whence he had come out. This was not a sudden thought, but the result of a deliberation consequent on his finding no rest. He looks in again at his old haunts. He there finds everything ready to receive him, and very inviting—empty, swept, and garnished. Something seems to say to him, "Enter again, and as of old every thing you desire shall be ministered to you." He does not resist. He enters. All the progress he had made is lost. The relapse is complete. Every one of us must in some matter or other have exhibited in himself such a picture as this. Remember that two reasons are suggested—that he found no rest in his new ways of life, and that he allowed his thoughts to go back to his old ways. He set his hand to the plough, but finding the work distasteful he looked back again to his former state of idleness; and then he gave over work. He expected an impossibility; that the new way would be immediately easy and pleasant. As well might you expect to learn any art or trade by wishing for a knowledge of it; or to find an oak-tree the growth of a night. Perseverance and prayer were the means by which the old man was to be exorcised, and the new man formed within him.

But the history is not yet all told; one more scene is presented to us, and that is the final one. No further struggle is made. The surrender is complete. The returning unclean spirit goes and takes to himself seven others, more wicked than himself; and they are all allowed to enter into the man's heart and dwell there. His last state is worse than his first; and so he ends. An army that has been thoroughly beaten and routed cannot renew the conflict. It has been demoralized and weakened by the defeat, and the enemy has become relatively much stronger.

The case resembles those of whom we are told "that it is impossible for them who were once enlightened; and have tasted of the heavenly gift, and were made partakers of the Holy Ghost; and have tasted the good word of God; and the powers of the world to come; if they shall fall away, to renew them again to repentance; seeing they crucify the Son of

God afresh, and put Him to an open shame." And again: "If we sin wilfully after that we have received the knowledge of the truth, there remaineth no more sacrifice for sin, but a certain looking for of judgment, and of fiery indignation." And so says St. Peter: "For it had been better for them not to have known the way of righteousness, than, after having known it to turn from the holy commandment delivered unto them. But it happened to them according to the true proverb; The dog is turned to his own vomit again, and the sow that was washed to her wallowing in the mire."

What can be more appalling! But I cannot leave the subject in this position. As a minister of the Word of God I must say that that Word contains statements that counteract the sense of dead hopelessness, and of blank despair which what has just been said would leave on the mind. How much, for instance, is there in the parable of the prodigal son to tell us of the inexhaustible, the infinite mercy, nay, love of God. And does not the idea pervade all Scripture, that our Father in heaven is not willing that any of His children should perish, but that all should come to Him, and that all should be saved? And we are told that the time will come when the Son shall have given up every thing to the Father; and so this dispensation shall have come to an end. And if it shall have come to an end, then we cannot believe that suffering and sin will remain as a residuum of it; for we need not believe that they existed before it, and independently of it. At all events, we are told that "God will be all in all." And if He shall be all in all, then there can be no more sin or suffering; or any thing to oppose itself to His will.

The distress of mind which arises at considering the Scripture that has been before us, must have been intended to arise. As this is its legitimate effect, it must have been intended. But neither may we forget the opposite conclusions which several particular statements of God's Word were equally intended to leave on the mind. And if any find a difficulty in reconciling these opposite, though I think not contradictory, truths, they must hold them both. When they think of themselves, they may dwell on the first. When they think of God they must dwell on the last. We know little now. We shall be able to reconcile them when we know all things even as we are now known of God.

Observations on the foregoing Sermon.

It is a difficult task to give in a sermon a continuous comment on a narrative used as text; especially when, as is generally the case with our Lord's parables, it is impossible to add any thing either to the clearness or forcibleness of the original. The reader must decide whether to his mind any thing has been gained in the case of the one before us by dividing the story into what may be compared to the acts of a drama, and endeavoring to connect each with the personal experience of the hearers.

I endeavor in the latter part of the sermon to avoid a mistake which many sermon-writers and commentators are apt to fall into; the mistake of supposing that their work is done when they have explained the meaning of the text and founded some exhortation upon it. It often happens that a very important part of their work still remains to be done, that of showing the relation in which the meaning of their text stands to other parts of Scripture which have a bearing upon it.

SERMON IV.

THE CENTURION OF CÆSAREA.

Acts x. 1, 2.

"There was a certain man in Cæsarea called Cornelius, a centurion of the band called the Italian band, a devout man, and one that feared God with all his house, which gave much alms to the people, and prayed to God alway."

This is the character given of the man who was the first to leave heathenism, and enter the Church of Christ. Some of us, as we heard it read, may have thought that it was the description of an ordinarily good and religious man; and of what might have been expected to be the conduct of such a one. And I shall endeavor to show why it is so; and that there is nothing accidental about any one of the particulars of his character, or of his conduct. We shall understand the man when we have made out the reasons that existed for what we are told of him, and seen the connection of the several statements.

We have just heard,[1] as the chapter from which our

[1] This sermon was preached on Dec. 10, 1865, on which day Acts x. is read as the Second Lesson for the Morning Service.

text is taken was read, that this first Gentile convert was admitted to the Christian Church by the Apostle Peter; and we saw that he would have been so unwilling to have done this that a miraculous interposition was needed to persuade him. And even after he had been commanded by a vision to undertake the work, he speaks in an apologetic tone of what he had come to do. Eight years had passed since his Lord had sent him forth to establish His kingdom, but Peter tells us he still rigidly observed the ceremonial law of Moses—he had never eaten any thing which according to that law was common or unclean. He asserts that it is an unlawful thing for a man that is a Jew to keep company with, or to come unto one of another nation; and he enters into explanations to justify himself for being engaged in receiving a Gentile into the Christian Church. Compare this with the way in which his fellow-Apostle Paul speaks of the same occurrence in the Scripture you have just heard read as the Epistle for the day.[2] He is all eagerness to justify the admission of the Gentiles; and to show from the Scriptures of the Old Dispensation that their admission had been originally, and all along intended. How hesitatingly does St. Peter make up his mind to receive Cornelius; how gladly would St. Paul have welcomed him! Whence this difference? Some perhaps may

[2] Rom. xv. 4. The Epistle for the Second Sunday in Advent.

be in the habit of supposing that in matters of this kind there neither was, nor could have been any difference between two Apostles. But what is thus in the Scriptures for this present service forced on our attention will correct us in this mistake. We may feel a little surprise at the discovery, and even a slight reluctance to acknowledge it; but as the surprise and reluctance were the result of a mistake, the discovery and acknowledgment of the mistake will be of advantage to us. We shall then see, what will impart a far more life-like interest to what we read in God's Word, that a man's having been called to become an Apostle did not obliterate his natural character; but that he became an Apostle, retaining the character he had previously possessed. See the character respectively of St. Peter and of St. Paul as reflected by their conduct in reference to the admission of the Gentiles. St. Peter evidently was a man who was capable of receiving new ideas, for he had received the Gospel of Jesus Christ; but he was at the same time a man who was incapable of giving up old ideas, for he could not abandon the ceremonial law in which he had been brought up, although the purpose of that law had now been served in bringing him to Christ. St. Paul, on the other hand, was a man who felt so strongly whatever he accepted, that he rejected whatever was opposed to it, however dearly he might previously have cherished it. When his faith was that of a Jew he would have destroyed all belief in Christ. No sooner was he converted to Christ than he gave himself up wholly to preaching the faith he formerly had persecuted. The observances of the law had no longer any attraction for him. There was no reservation in his feelings. What he felt he felt with all his heart. What he did he did with all his might. He would straightway have the old typical and ceremonial observances abolished utterly; and the Gospel, pure and simple, preached to every creature. To suppose that all the instruments we find employed by God in the establishment of the Gospel were brought precisely to the same state of mind, renders it impossible for us to understand much that is recorded in the sacred page itself; and also deprives us of one fertile source of interest in reading it—that which arises from the contemplation of the varieties of human character and feelings as they exhibit themselves in the working out of the great purpose.

But what I have now to speak to you about is the description given of Cornelius, and how that came to be the character of the man who was selected as the first-fruits to Christ of all the Gentile world.

We are told first of all that he was "a devout man." The thought probably that is called up in the minds of many as they hear this said is that of devoutness as we see it around us, and feel it in ourselves, that is to say, we think of a man being devout as a

Christian. We think of Christian devoutness. To some it may even sound strange and novel to have any other kind suggested to them. But devoutness, or a sense of the existence of God, and of the relation in which man stands towards Him, is one of the constituent elements of the common mental or spiritual nature of man. In some it is stronger, and more enlightened than in others—that is all the difference. It exists in all men, to speak generally. In all times it has existed. It has been found, and is still to be found, among all races of men. It is an instinct of the heart and of the reason of man. As the Apostle reminds us, God revealed Himself to men's understandings by His works and His dispensations. Of the heathen especially he says this. The fruitful seasons God sent appealed to their feelings of gratitude and of dependence. And long before the Apostle's time it had been noted that there was a voice in the starry firmament which had gone out into all lands, and had been heard by all people; and which they had understood as speaking to them of God. Into whatever heathen land you may go, in every city you will find costly temples raised to express the devoutness of its inhabitants. So was it of old time. And now well-nigh all that meets the eye of bygone empires and states of civilization are the remains of their magnificent temples. These are standing witnesses, and witnesses that cannot deceive, of the devoutness of all races of men in all times and places. We know the mind of Cornelius's countrymen, and we know that devoutness was a very large element in the constitution of their inner nature.

But we may go further than the contemplation of the outward manifestations of this universal sentiment. True, it is not religion as we understand religion, but it is the foundation of religion, so much so that religion could not exist without it any more than a temple could be raised without a foundation, or a tree grow and be kept alive without its roots. The sense we have of God, and of the relation in which we stand towards Him, is the foundation, the root of religion. Take it away and there is nothing to work upon, nothing to rest upon. Or we may look at it in another way, as the seed, the germ out of which, under the favoring and progressive circumstances God ordains, religion, even that of the Gospel of Jesus Christ, is in fulness of time developed; for God ordains suitable circumstances for the growth of religion just as He does for the growth of a plant.

You will not then understand the nature of man, or the history of religion, or the character of this man, and both of the former throw light upon the latter, unless you understand that devoutness is an attribute of man, and belongs to the heathen as well as to Christians. Now Cornelius had been devout as a heathen: indeed it was this disposition, while he was still in heathenism, that brought him to entertain the consideration of a purer and higher form of religion than that of his own country in which he had been brought up. You must separate in him the idea of devoutness from the idea of the approximations he made to the highest and purest religion. The former existed before the latter in his mind, just as it had done in the world. It was the former that brought him to the latter. And having done this great work for him, it did not leave him, or die out of his mind. On the contrary; it became purified and exalted, and a still more vivifying and active principle. His faith in Christ would without its continuance have been but ineffective and dead; while with it that faith lived, and moved, and had being. But again I say the two things are quite distinct. Devoutness is one of the ingredients of man's nature that is common to all; it is not only a necessary Christian quality, but it is also a good heathen quality. The first Gentile convert to Christ while still in heathenism had been a devout man.

And now we pass to another stage in the formation of his religious character. "He gave much alms to the people." This was not a heathen, assuredly not a Roman practice. Heathenism, and especially Roman heathenism, was intensely selfish. It was the character of the Government and of the people. They respected power and wealth; they had no commiseration for the suffering and the abject. Woe was with them the lot of the fallen. Man need not trouble himself to pity those whom God had forsaken. The Roman never founded institutions for the relief of the distressed in mind, body, or estate. With reference to this particular compare the past with the present. Perhaps in no city of the world of the same size as modern Christian Rome, and in no other country in the world with a population equal to that of modern Christian Italy, are there so many who live by alms. In this we have an abuse of one of the great principles of Christianity; but in heathen Rome it was most markedly the very reverse of this. In that hard-hearted city the beggar was little known in the time of Cornelius. The word so seldom occurs in the literature of that age that the character itself must have been very rare. This could not have been because there were none in a state of destitution, no abjects (they must have abounded in such a city), but because it would have been useless for the abject and the destitute to have appealed to feelings that did not exist. How then came this Roman captain to have acquired the habit of giving much alms?

There is no difficulty in answering the question. It was from his acquaintance with that religion which through Moses, David, and the prophets God had given to the people among whom Cornelius had been for some time residing. "He was a just man who feared God," that is now, the God of Israel, "and was of good report among all the nation of the Jews." It is the Master who tells us, and we find it laid down in the law itself, that the highest regard we can practically feel for others, is just the very principle of the law; for it is in the Book of Leviticus that we first meet with the great saying, which Jesus recalls in His conversation with the lawyer, "that thou shouldest love thy neighbor as thyself." Cornelius was now well acquainted with this law and its principles. He had received it as a revelation of God, and from God. He had formed his religion from it. The Jewish law, in a way in which no heathen law ever had done, charged itself with the care of the orphan and the widow, of those who had none to help them, of the poor, the maimed, the destitute, and the stranger. We see this every where in the Law, the Psalms, and the Prophets. Cornelius's idea therefore of the duty of man towards his fellow-man, regarded as a matter of religion, was, in conformity with this teaching, to love his fellow-man, and gladly to do for those who needed his assistance, all that love can suggest. This is the principle which fulfils the Law.

That this was the principle of the Jewish Law well-nigh alone proves its divine origin. You must recollect that that Law was promulgated in a rude and violent age, and intended for a rude and unmanageable people, insomuch that many of its enactments were adapted to such a state of things. How marvellous then that this principle of love, so widely at variance with the tone and with the circumstances of the times, and so immeasurably in advance of the legislation and of the feeling of the most polished nations of the heathen world, should have been made its governing idea. And now this principle coming to Cornelius through the channel of the Jewish Law, commended itself to him as the rule of his feelings towards, and of his dealings with, his fellow-men. The very word I last used contained an idea absolutely new to him. He had not been brought up to regard men, considered as men, in the light of his fellows. He, a Roman, had not thought the inhabitants of subject nations, or that part of the population that was in slavery, or the poor of his own country, as in any sense his fellows, as having claims upon him, and as entitled to be treated by him with consideration and respect. But now the hard selfish arrogance of the Roman was abandoned, and his feelings and practice had risen to the level of the Jewish Law. To be merciful, to be compassionate, to give, he felt to be his duty to man as required by God. "He gave much alms to the poor.

His devoutness, then, and his alms-giving mark two stages in his religious progress: his devoutness the stage when he was religious as a good heathen might be; his alms-giving when he had superadded to the devoutness of a good heathen the religious sense of duty to others which the Jewish Law prescribed.

To each of these stages is appended a single illustration which we must notice as we pass along in the consideration of this good man's character. He was a devout man, "who feared God with all his house;" and the subsequent parts of the history show more than this, for we have indications of others beside those of his own house having been influenced by his devoutness. "The devout soldier," who we know was among those who waited on him continually, and whom he sent with his two servants to Joppa to summon Peter, may have been intended to be included among "those of his house." But to meet Peter he invites his kinsfolk and acquaintance, who he knows are in the same state of mind, and who, we cannot but think, must have been brought into it by his influence. Real devoutness, since we all of us have already some amount of it in our nature, is very infectious. Not only does it pass from one mind to other minds, because those other minds are predisposed by what they have of their own to admit it, but it consciously makes the effort thus to spread and propagate itself. And this is an indication of true devoutness, that this effort is made, and that it is made successfully. A devout man will generally have, as Cornelius had, a devout household, and devout kinsfolk and acquaintance.

The illustration which is appended to the description of the second stage of his religious progress, is that he prayed to God always. This is inseparably connected with his giving much alms. For, remark, it is not merely that he prayed—he had done that in his state of devout heathenism—but that he prayed to God; the one true God, by whom he had been taught to love his neighbor as himself. His desire was to commune with that Being from whom he had learnt this most blessed principle, and so to drink more largely of His Spirit. Each implies the other. If he gave much alms, he would pray to God always; and if he prayed to God always, he would give much alms.

But to proceed to the third and last stage of his character. This devout man who had brought others to fear God,—this man who gave much alms and prayed to God always,—had still one step to take. But it may be said what more could he have needed? Is there not enough of religion in what has been already said of him? Is he not already all that a religious man can desire to be? Does any reasonable want still remain unsatisfied? Yes: the greatest need, the most pressing want of all that religion is concerned with, has still to be supplied. What he wants is precisely that which all religions, more or less dimly, or more or less distinctly, aim at. He wants that which all the altars, all the temples, and all the services throughout the world were designed as instruments for attaining, but which none, not even the sacrifices and services of the Jewish Temple, could completely supply. He wants something that will meet and remove the sense of sin, of unworthiness before God, of alienation from Him, even of contradiction to Him. He wants a sense of pardon, of acceptance, of reconciliation. This can be obtained only through what Peter has to communicate to him; the Gospel of our Lord and Saviour Jesus Christ, "through whom alone we obtain remission of our sins;" Christ, the Saviour, was what Peter preached to him. We have the narrative of what passed on the occasion; we know what Peter said. He spoke of Christ, and of Christ only, as the Great Deliverer that had been ex pected. And we know in what way Cornelius received what Peter said of Christ.

Here then was a third and distinct state in the religious progress of this first Gentile convert. There was now superadded to the two conditions of mind he had previously arrived at, that at which they had aimed, and that for which in the religious progress of the human race they had been the preparation—a sense of forgiveness and acceptance, accompanied with, nay almost arising out of, a clear perception of the goodness and loving-kindness of our Father in heaven; a far clearer perception than was possible under the old dispensation, where God was revealed chiefly as the Lawgiver and Judge of a rude and stubborn people. And consequently there was now made a fuller and more direct appeal than was formerly possible to the good and loving qualities God has implanted in the heart; and the faith that works by love, not obedience extorted from fear, became the principle of the spiritual life. This was the wisdom that came down from above. It brought into the foreground a gentler and more heavenly view of duty, one element of which was that sense of universal brotherhood in which we see even the Apostle Peter had been so deficient. This was what Cornelius, and after him the civilized world, gained by rising to a belief in Christ the Light and the Saviour of the world, for He cannot be our Saviour any more than He can be our Light, without our knowing and feeling it, and being assured of it.

And what I have been endeavoring to set before you is, my good friends, not merely an interesting picture of a bygone state of things. What passed so many hundred years ago in the mind and heart of this Centurion of the Italian band, is a picture of what passes just as distinctly in our own minds and hearts. Every one of us who is in the habit of coming here to God's House is more or less devout. That it is that impels us to come. Some of us give large alms to the poor. Some also have arrived at that full assurance of faith, which gives them "hope, and peace, and joy in believing." But some stop at the first state. It seems to them like religion. They fear and respect God. But, my friends, you who have gone no further than this state are not yet Christians. You have advanced no further than the good heathen had. This you may think a hard saying. But look at the history of Cornelius's religion, and you will understand what is meant. If you are pained at the statement, it will not have been said unprofitably. There are others again, and these are a very numerous class, who go no further than the second stage. Here they feel sure is practical religion. Here is palpable proof of their having submitted themselves to the teaching of God. They are keeping the Law of Love even as expounded and enlarged by Jesus Christ. They are doing good. They are diminishing the misery that is around them. They visit the fatherless and the widow in their distress. They feed the hungry; they clothe the naked. This is practical religion. But, my friends, this is only the stage which Cornelius had reached when his knowledge did not go beyond an acquaintance with the Law of the first Dispensation. If this be enough, then was it superfluous that Jesus Christ should have come, and taught, and suffered. You must go up higher. There is a third, the last and crowning stage. You must go to Christ. You must learn of Him. You must cast your burden upon Him. So shall you find rest unto your soul. That will be a state in which your love for Him who so loved you as to give Himself for you, will have cast out fear. You will be conscious of God's love for you; and you will no longer be conscious of the existence of any bar to your loving Him. This I trust is the state of some among us. We cannot say who are Christ's in this sense. Nor can we say who among us are resting on the heathen, and who on the Judaical form of religiousness. Each must try and examine himself as in the sight of God who knows the heart.

Observations on the foregoing Sermon.

I wrote the foregoing sermon for this work on the Monday after I preached it. I had previously to preaching it made only a mental study of what I was to say. I have put it on paper for the purpose of showing, if possible, how analysis, and its opposite, comprehensiveness of view, and how, too, historical matter, may be used in order to give interest and distinctiveness to a familiar subject; and this to such a degree as to enable the preacher to bring home his discourse in an intelligible and forcible manner to the understandings and consciences of the congregation. By analysis, I here mean the distinction drawn between the three states of the religious heathen, the religious Jew, and the Christian; by comprehensiveness of view, the reference made to the manner in which the religious sentiment shows itself in all ages and nations; by historical matter, the reference made to the Jewish law and to Roman history.

I have also another motive for giving it just as I preached it. I had intended to say something about the proof my subject gives us, fortified by that of the other Centurion, whose faith was greater than that which Jesus had found in any in Israel, that even the profession of a Roman soldier in the tributary province of Judea, those whom John advised to be content with their pay, and not to accuse any falsely, might be sanctified by religion unto a discipline for the practice of duty both to God and man. This was what I had intended. But being struck by the indications which the Scriptures read in the Service supplied of the difference in feeling between the Apostles Peter and Paul on the very subject I was about to speak upon, the admission of the Gentiles to the Church, I thought it better not to lose the opportunity presented for pointing out this difference. It was the 10th of December, and the second Sunday in Advent; and the difference in feeling between St. Peter in the second lesson, the 10th of the Acts of the Apostles, and St. Paul in the Epistle, from the 15th of his Epistle to the Romans, was most obvious. I thought it better to drop something I had intended to say, and instead to call the attention to this point, not merely because it was closely connected with the fact I was about to speak upon, but because at the same time it presented an excellent opportunity for saying a few words on a subject which throws some light upon the nature of Inspiration; and which besides gives a more life-like interest to what we read in God's Word.

Now it is plain that I could have made no use of this opportunity, which was of much value both exegetically, and because it connected the sermon very closely with the foregoing parts of the Service, if I had been a reader of written sermons.

But as my object is to give my younger brethren hints for the proper composition of sermons, I will further remark that my having done this injured the proper effect of the sermon, because it introduced what was in reality irrelevant matter; that is, matter which was only connected with my subject, and not necessary for its elucidation; and so far it was destructive of that oneness of purpose which ought to pervade all that is said in a sermon. The advantage however of saying it outweighed this disadvantage, and so I introduced it. And remark that it was out of place not only because it was unnecessary for the elucidation of the subject, but also because, being in itself a point of much interest, it impressed itself too much on the mind at the expense of the real subject of the discourse.

With respect to the references to history which this sermon contains, I would observe that nothing of that kind is of any value in what is addressed to uneducated persons. As they cannot understand such matters, they are only confused and wearied by the mention of them.

In writing this sermon the day after I had preached it, I was struck with the difficulty, I almost found it the impossibility, of maintaining that continuity of thought which comes spontaneously in speaking. The length of time required to write a sentence, and the attention requisite for the work of the pen, are constantly breaking the direct stream of thought, and diverting it into side channels. This is worthy of being noticed as a disadvantage of writing in comparison with speaking. One's style also in speaking is more homogeneous.

In the foregoing sermon it was necessary to point out that the germ of the religious character of the Centurion was his devoutness; but the word is repeated too often, and too much is made of the fact. I leave this uncorrected, that it may illustrate a fault.

SERMON V.

THE CENTURION OF CAPERNAUM.

MATTHEW viii. 10. 13.

"When Jesus heard it, He marvelled, and said to them that followed, Verily, I have not found so great faith, no, not in Israel. And Jesus said unto the Centurion, Go thy way; and as thou hast believed, so be it done unto thee."

THERE are four Centurions of whom in the Gospels and Acts of the Apostles very honorable mention is made. First comes this Centurion of Capernaum, whose faith was greater than that of any in Israel. He is followed by the Centurion who, being a spectator of the Crucifixion, declared his belief that He who had just expired on the Cross was truly the Son of God; a conviction which certainly at that moment does not appear to have existed in the mind of any one of the disciples. The next was the Centurion who was the first of all the Gentile world to be admitted to the Church of Christ. Again, it was a Centurion who saved the Apostle Paul from being thrown out the ship into the sea in the storm off Melita; an act, the effect of which will for ever be felt in the Church to the extent in which it contributed to strengthen the Pauline element in the setting forth of the Gospel.

What is told us of these Centurions reminds us, by the way, how illiberal and unjust it is to condemn a man on account of the profession to which he belongs. There are men, in these days even, who speak disparagingly of those who belong to the profession of arms. With how much more reason might this have been done of the officers of the Roman army, which was very notorious, particularly in subject countries such as Judæa then was, for rapacity, arrogance, and cruelty; and yet here are four officers of that army conspicuous for piety, for openness to conviction, and for a proper sense of duty and humanity, at a time when well-nigh every one around them was overpowered by superstitious terrors, or had abandoned himself to disbelief of all religion. The same remark must be made of class prejudices. The rich think disparagingly of, and distrust the poor; and just in the same way do the poor regard the rich. This is narrow-minded and sinful. The religiously wise, and the worldly wise too, will estimate a man not by considering the demerits of others, but by endeavoring to ascertain what is the character, but more particularly what are the merits of the man himself. It is a mistake to suppose that it shows like wide experience to condemn whole professions and classes. Wide experience that has been profited by teaches that there are no two persons alike; and that even in those whose faults are very prominent there is still good to be found by all who have the eyes to see it.

But to come to our Centurion. He had been brought up in all the abominations and wickednesses of heathenism; but he has now built a synagogue for the promotion of the knowledge of the true God. From what darkness had he passed into what marvellous light! We can hardly imagine the conflicts that must have taken place in his thoughts and feelings, while he was breaking away from the immemorial religion of his country, under which it had grown from a small city into the mistress of the world; and while he was being brought to know God through the sacred books of one of the most despised and hated of all the subject nations of the empire. But just as the wise man will recognize moral worth whatever be the calling or class of its possessor, so also will he be disposed to recognize truth whatever may be the means through which it may be presented to him; and he will hold his mind in readiness to abandon falsehood, however strongly it may be able to commend itself to his feelings, his interests, or his habits of thought. The struggle may involve the very tearing out of his heart-strings, but in proportion to the nobility of his nature will be the singleness of his desire that the truth only should triumph within him.

But the struggle was now over; and we have to see in what it had issued. First look at his liberality. To those among whom he was then residing he had given a synagogue. This, recent investigations show, was a costly act. There are several motives which may prompt us to give; I need only notice two here. A man may regard giving as a substitute for religion; or genuine religion may impel him to give. It is often said depreciatingly, Giving is not religion. The reply is, No; but there can be no religion without it. The religion of Christ would have men ready to give, wherever an occasion presents itself, their money, their time, their thought, even their own selves. Take the mere giving of money; he that is of the spirit of Christ will always find happiness in giving, because the promotion of a good object will be dearer to him than his money. How many are there in these days amongst ourselves who have exactly followed in the steps of this good man's liberality. They have assisted in restoring or building some house of God, or have carried through the whole work at their own sole cost. The thing done gave them greater pleasure than the retention of what it cost would have given them.

And now notice this Centurion's piety. It showed itself in every way in which it could have been possible for him to make it operative on the minds and hearts of others; that is, in his life and conversation, in all that he said and did. But here I confine my observations to the one particular just mentioned: he had built a synagogue for the Jews of Capernaum. Piety, if genuine, must endeavor to propagate itself as diffusively as possible. How this was to be done by himself must have been the question which above all others occupied his mind. Of course it is to be propagated most widely through the instrumentality of letters. The man for instance who writes a book such as that of Thomas à Kempis, *On the Imitation of Christ;* or that of Jeremy Taylor on *Holy Living and Dying*, kindles and feeds the flame of piety in a manner which can be effected by no other means. He works without being subject to the restrictions of time or place. This is the mighty prerogative of the highest form of intellectual work. It is unapproachable by any other means. It was not given to this Roman Centurion, it is not given to one of a million, perhaps not to one in a whole generation of the human race to work in this way. But he did what was in his power, and what, though at a long interval, came next in effectiveness; he built a house of God, a place where the Word of God might week after week, year after year, and generation after generation be set forth by reading, by exposition, by exhortation. He could establish a centre where religious thought and feeling might be cultivated for that neighborhood while he was there, and after he was gone: and that was what he did, and what he meant to do when he built the people of Capernaum a synagogue.

Observe next the kindliness and considerateness of his character. It was this that brought him before Jesus, and gave him a place in the records of the Gospel history. He is very solicitous for the recovery or the relief of a poor grievously palsied slave. In what strong contrast does this stand with the feelings that were usual among his countrymen on such subjects! About their aged or worn-out slaves they were notoriously careless and hard-hearted. They called them and treated them as cattle. But this man begs the chief people of the city to go to Jesus and beseech Him to restore to health the poor creature. His feelings are an anticipation of Christian charity.

Another particular which the history brings out is his humility. He deems himself unworthy either of going to Jesus, or of having Jesus come to him. Here again we shall fall short of a proper view of the character and merits of the man if we content ourselves with the thought that he possessed those feelings which we understand by the word humility. As in the former particular, we must contrast what he had become with the ideas in which he had been brought up. His arrogant countrymen had no conception of this grace. They had no word in their language for it, regarded as an adornment and excellence of character. With them it was a vice of the mind and heart; something mean and contemptible. The fact is, that it can only exist in those who have some knowledge of God, and of themselves, and of what God requires of them. What now so much becomes him is just what he would formerly have shrunk from as un-Roman and despicable.

And consider too how what in him, because he had been brought up in heathenism, and was a Roman soldier, had been positive vices were now changed into negative excellences. I pass by the probability that he had been a man who would have borne malice, and would have deceived, but that it was impossible now that he could do either. There are other points on which we may speak with more certainty. What we call debauchery and profligacy were of the very routine of heathen life. We know how frequently the Apostle Paul refers to this source of the corruption of heathenism. But the life of this good man could not any longer have been tainted with this kind of impurity. Again, we recollect what the Baptist's advice was to the soldiers who came to ask him what they should do. "They were not to accuse any falsely, and they were to be content with their wages." This implies how much they had it in their power to oppress the subject population, and how frequently they availed themselves of their opportunities of this kind. But this man did not extort and oppress.

Great then were his negative merits as well as his positive virtues. We naturally ask if it is possible to trace them up to any adequate cause? Yes, the cause was what Christ particularizes and speaks so highly of: He had not found so great faith; no, not in Israel. It is so among ourselves. A man's character,—and if his character, then of course his conduct,—is the result of what he believes. It is not only, as it was in his case, and as it will be in the case of every one of us, "as thou hast believed, so be it done unto thee," but also, as thou hast believed, so wilt thou do.

This faith is needed by all, even the most learned; and is possible to all, even the most unlearned. Those most learned need it because it does not consist in learning, but in a sense of our relation to God. And because it does not consist in learning, but in what God has placed within the reach of every one He has made accountable for his conduct, it is attainable by the unlearned.

Christ's comparison of the faith of the Centurion with that of the chosen and highly-favored people, and the way in which He marked his approval by granting what the man asked for, convey to us the lesson that is it not our gifts and opportunities that will ultimately be of advantage to us; our having possessed them may even increase our condemnation; what will benefit and save us is the use we shall have made of them. On this subject two questions must be asked. First, What is the talent the Lord of all has entrusted to me? and then, Am I using it so as to promote His glory, to benefit others, and to improve myself?

I have one more thought to set before you. Compare this Centurion in his life, and in the end of his life, with the other Centurions at that time in the Roman army. We can imagine what they were. The great majority, of course, were as the great majority always have been. They gave themselves little trouble about themselves. As they had been brought up, so they lived, and so they died. Some, however, made use of their opportunities to enrich themselves dishonestly and cruelly, at the cost of the provincials. Some by attention to their professional duties rose to high military appointments. Some may have returned to Rome, and by endeavoring to serve the state at home became great in civil capacities. This man loved those among whom he resided, and was loved by them in return. He was liberal. He was intelligently religious. He was considerate and kind to his poor slave. He thought humbly of himself. He had faith in God. He believed in Jesus Christ. I do not say that the lines which were adopted by his brother-Centurions were without any reward in this world; but I affirm that the happiness conferred on him by the line he adopted was well worth having. There is One who has told us that it will be rewarded in this world an hundredfold, and will lead to life everlasting in the world to come. Each must consider, and choose for himself, what he thinks best. May God help us in making our choice.

Observations on the foregoing Sermon.

I began this sermon with the mention of the four Centurions, because what we have to say of them is of so much interest that it must at once engage the attention of the hearers.

This mention of them gives an opportunity, which is made use of in the second paragraph, for awakening in the minds of the congregation a sense of the injustice of the common fault of condemning whole classes and professions, a fault that is as unchristian as it is common. This practice pretends to be the result of experience, whereas experience of mankind, in those who are able to understand its lessons, is just what will most effectually save us from it. In the Sacred History we have good Pharisees and good Publicans, as well as good Roman soldiers. Jesus came from Nazareth. A good opportunity for making people feel the foolishness and wickedness of this practice ought not to be lost, although it is not a matter that belongs to a sermon on the character of this Centurion. But it springs naturally from the joint mention of the four Centurions, which was the point from which I started.

The graces which are manifested in this Centurion's character ought not merely to be catalogued. To bring them out distinctively, and to unite them into a portrait of the man, must be the aim of the sermon of which he is the subject. Each should be so presented as not only to make its nature apparent, but also to awaken interest, and to engender in the hearer the feeling that it is worth having and seeking. The more connectedly they are all presented, the more distinctness and life will it give to the Centurion's character.

The comparison of the works of Thomas à Kempis and Jeremy Taylor with the building of a synagogue would revive flagging attention; and would induce the congregation to make an estimate, and, too, a deservedly high one, of the Centurion's gift to the people of Capernaum, as a means for promoting piety. Without some stimulus or assistance of this kind the minds of the hearers would not be disposed to make any estimate of its value at all.

What the Centurion had escaped in abandoning heathenism, and what he had gained in coming to

God through the Law and through Christ, must be indicated, for without this we can form no real conception of the man; but it must not be dwelt on at any length, because the character of the man, and not the difference between heathenism and the knowledge of God, is the subject of the sermon.

The exhortation is contained indirectly in the last paragraph. This is a case where an indirect way of submitting a consideration is more forcible than the direct way would have been. The direct way of putting the exhortation would have been to say: "You see what this man was. You see what he gained. Become like him. Secure what he secured." This would have been very common-place and feeble. But by giving a comparative view of the aims and principles, of the modes of life and probable success in life of this man and his brother-Centurions, the hearers are enabled to see distinctly what is the object of the sermon, without being directly told; and they will feel that their approval of the man's character, and their desire that their last end should be like his, are results of their own judgment.

SERMON VI.

THE SENSE OF SIN AND THE SENSE OF DUTY LEAD TO FAITH.

LUKE iii. 10–14.

"And the people asked him, saying, What shall we do then? He answereth and saith unto them, He that hath two coats, let him impart to him that hath none; and he that hath meat let him do likewise. Then came also publicans to be baptized, and said unto him, Master, what shall we do? And he said unto them, Exact no more than that which is appointed you. And the soldiers likewise demanded of him, saying, And what shall we do? And he said unto them, Do violence to no man, neither accuse any falsely; and be content with your wages."

THE endeavor to do our duty stands in two relations towards faith. In that which is most frequently insisted on it springs from faith and is its consequence. In the other the position of the two is just reversed, and the endeavor to do our duty appears as the cause of faith. This is the relation between them supposed in the Scripture of which my text forms a part, and which I now propose to bring before you.

In order that this may be seen, we must recall the circumstances under which the questions contained in our text were asked and answered. Jesus had not yet entered on His ministry. John, His appointed forerunner, was preparing the minds of the people for believing on Him. The burden of his preaching was, "Prepare ye the way of the Lord." Mark then how he endeavors to prepare them for believing on Christ, when Christ should Himself come forward and proclaim His divine mission. He does it by awakening within them the sense of sin and the sense of duty. His preaching is described in one word when we are told that he called upon them "to repent." Cease to do evil, learn to do well; otherwise you will be incapable of believing on the Great and Holy One who is shortly about to appear before you.

What followed is interesting as well as instructive. It was what is contained in our text. His appeals to the sense of duty and the sense of sin had come home to the conscience of his hearers. It was not the camel's-hair garments and the leathern girdle he wore, nor the locusts and wild honey he ate, nor his dwelling in the wilderness that moved them. These things were in the eyes of John's hearers just what the clerical dress is amongst ourselves. They merely indicated that he had undertaken the office of a teacher of religion. Eastern ideas have always required in such persons some such austerities. What moved them was not what met the eye, but what had through their ears passed to their hearts and consciences. God has made every man more or less capable of being wrought up to a desire for what is pure and holy, and to a dislike of what is sinful. And John having excited these feelings among his audience, just in the manner in which they might be excited amongst ourselves, they severally inquire of him, "What they shall do." His object in exciting these feelings, and in the replies he made to their questions, was to bring them to Christ. This we must bear in mind while we review the scene.

First the general multitude ask him, "What shall we do?" Mark, he could not say as Paul said to the jailer at Philippi, "Believe on the Lord Jesus Christ, and thou shalt be saved;" for the Lord Jesus Christ had not yet manifested Himself to the world. John was at that very moment preparing them for receiving Him. With this then in view, what is the advice he gives them? He singles out the one commandment which is of universal application, and tells them to be considerate and helpful to one another. And to make his meaning as palpable as possible, and to prevent its being lost in vague generalities, he puts his reply in the form of two instances: "Let him," he says, "who has two coats, impart to him who has none; and let him who has meat, do likewise." To the mixed multitude then he recommends, as a preparation for belief in Christ, the most general of all duties. And as this duty does not rest merely on the fact that it is enjoined by religion, but is enjoined by religion because a foundation for it had all along been laid in the higher and better sentiments of our nature, his recommendation would find an echo in the hearts of all those his preaching had already awakened in some degree to a sense of sin and a sense of duty. If he could induce them to act on these feelings by putting in practice his recommendation, he knew that he would thus be leading them to Christ.

And when the farmers of the taxes saw that he was ready to give advice to those who sought it they also asked him, "And what shall we do?" Again see, bearing in mind what he was aiming at, how he endeavors to attain his aim. How apposite, too, and how full of good sense, is his advice. There is nothing vague, sentimental, or fanatical about it. Now he has to deal with a particular class; and he bids them guard against that particular sin, for the commission of which their particular calling presented especial opportunities and temptations. He says, "Exact no more than that which is appointed you." It was frequently in their power to practise these unjust exactions. Things of this kind were not looked into very closely; so long as the Government received the rent at which they had let out the taxes, and so long as there were no public disturbances, all was right. In collecting these taxes there were seen behind the farmers the armed force and the tribunals of the Romans. This gave these men great facilities for exacting more than was appointed. The victims of their cruel and dishonest impositions would be indisposed and afraid to go into the courts of their foreign oppressors, which they could hardly hope would be courts of justice to them in such cases.—We know that it was the general practice of the farmers of the taxes in Judæa to sin in this way. Having awakened then in these persons the sense of sin and the sense of duty, he dexterously turns these feelings upon the point where in their case reform was most needed, and with respect to which their requickening consciences would be most sensitive, trusting that, if he could induce them to undertake what he recommended, he would in that way bring them to Christ.

Let us go on with this instructive scene. When he had answered the publicans, the soldiers came forward with a similar request. Again in framing his reply he had in view the same object as before, that of bringing the inquirers to Christ; and he takes the same ground, that of the temptations which most beset them. "My advice," he says, "to you soldiers is, that you do violence to no man, neither accuse any falsely; and that you be content with your wages." This would not be suitable advice to the soldiers of our own army; but it was the most appropriate that could have been given to the soldiers who were then standing before John, and whose consciences had just been touched by his exhortations. They were probably heathen soldiers in a conquered country, and so were not likely to be very strictly amenable to law. It would frequently happen that they would plunder, and practise various kinds of oppression towards the subject population, which they hated and despised, especially by threats of false accusations of hostility to the Government, and of the breach of various regulations that had been imposed on them by their conquerors. "You have become conscious," he says, "of having committed these particulars kinds of wickedness. Endeavor from this moment to avoid them."

Such then was the Baptist's method of preparing in these people's hearts the way of the Lord. It consisted in persuading them to give up their common besetting sins, and to undertake their common everyday duties.

And now to bring this home to ourselves. Possibly there may be some here present who have scarcely any more distinct faith in Jesus Christ than John's hearers had. How shall I, Christ's Minister among them, endeavor to put them upon a way by which they may attain to this faith? This, as a Minister of God's Word, must be my great aim, my paramount object. Some might say, "Recommend prayer." But I know that men cannot pray who have not faith. Others might say, "Speak of the wrath of God against sin, and of the grace of our Lord Jesus Christ." But, again, what is needed is to bring men to believe in these things. I am reduced then to that which the Scripture before us suggests—the effort to awaken men to a sense of duty, and a desire to perform it, and to a consciousness of their besetting sins, such as may give rise to the desire to escape from them.

You have, then, some belief in a connection between your present life and a life to come. To some extent you believe that the purpose of your existence is moral and spiritual, and not merely material. You have some apprehension of your having a Great Unseen Master, whose eye is ever upon you, and who is requiring of you certain dispositions and a certain mode of life. You do not feel these thoughts now for the first time stirring within you; you know that you are concerned in the matters to which they refer. But let us go more into particulars. You are a parent or a child, a husband or a wife, a master or a servant, a neighbor, or, to take the instances of the text, one of the multitude, a man among men, or a soldier, or a public functionary of some kind or other. Consider what belongs to and what grows out of your position; its calls, its opportunities, its temptations. You do not think that your position has no duties;

you do not think that it is a matter of indifference to your conscience how those duties are performed, or whether they are performed or not. Now imagine yourself endeavoring earnestly to do your duty as a parent, or master, or servant, or merely as a man among men, and cannot you see that this endeavor, as the herald of the Saviour saw, will lead you on to faith in that Saviour? Without Christian faith you feel and acknowledge that you have duties. The only logical inference is that you should endeavor to practise those duties. That attempt will probably issue in Christian faith.

See why it is so. It is an attempt which, as soon as a man begins to make it, he finds beset with difficulties. One want, which the hundredth, perhaps, as well as the ninety and nine will immediately feel, will be that of distinct and infallible authority for the kind of life he is entering on; and he will feel that it must be some authority external to himself. This is a very material point. There is a craving for certainty which is not to be found in one's self. Whence then is it to be obtained? The more a man looks into himself, the less confidence will he have in himself; the more distinctly will he perceive that he is misled by what he desires, by self-love, by prejudices, by his natural biasses, and also by his ignorance. The educated classes may think that they are more or less raised above these influences, these disturbing causes, or, rather, each may think so of himself; but does he think so of his friends and neighbors, as well instructed as himself? As respects, however, these subjects, who are we to consider as the educated classes? Even in those parts of the world which are intellectually the most advanced, they form a very small proportion of the whole. And if we extend our view to mankind generally, they become so small a proportion that they need hardly be taken into account. What we want all the while is something by which the great mass of mankind may be guided. Take any one from the passing crowd: this is what he needs. Look at the human race: this is what it needs. The impulses of the sense of duty, whether awakened from without or by a conscious effort, require sanction, and support, and guidance. These must be external. There must be something that speaks as it were with the voice of law—something authoritative.

Who then is there that can speak to us with this necessary authority, and with a voice that will be to us as the voice of law? Not the Scribes and Pharisees—they who sit in Moses' seat; not you, nor I, nor any other man. What any man may say on these subjects (subjects which do not admit of demonstration) must be more or less colored by the peculiarities of the individual, of the age in which he lives, and of the people to whom he belongs. Men can only see these things with imperfect vision through distorting media. The conclusion any individual may come to on these subjects is only what he thinks; it is his opinion, and must partake more or less of the nature of a conjecture or a guess. All the while what is wanted is certainty; for what is wanted is a rule that a man may live and die by. The philosophies of the ancients failed among other reasons from this, that they were not possessed of the requisite authority. One was arrayed against another; and all wore the aspect of guesses; whereas what was wanted was certainty. Whence then, and how, shall we obtain it? In this matter little or nothing can be done without it. The history of the human race shows that it can be obtained only from one source, that is, from Him who alone can speak with authority, to Whom alone in this matter authority and certainty belong, God Himself, the author of the moral law. It was this feeling that brought Christendom, and will naturally bring every one of us who shall have become desirous of discharging his duty, to the Word of God, that is, to the Incarnate Word—the Lord Jesus Christ, whom God sent to be in this particular the Light of the world, to give light to every man who desires light. He alone speaks not as men speak, but with authority and certainty.

As soon as this want is felt, we see that recourse is had to the Word of God, and to those who have made the Word of God their study. This is an ever-acting motive which generation after generation fills the house of God; which from the Apostles' days to our own has brought together so many Christian congregations—the desire to be told, albeit through a human channel, what God would have them to do. Nothing of the kind would ever have taken place if preachers spoke with no other authority than their own.

And if we pass from the sense of duty to that with which it is very closely connected, the sense of the relation that exists between man and the author of the moral law, we find precisely the same want felt, that of distinct and certain knowledge, derived from an authoritative source. Many put themselves forward as teachers in these times, as many have done in all times. But of all these could we accept one, Revelation entirely set aside, as capable of being the instructor of his brethren on this subject? Can the people of this country be each to himself a light upon this subject, or can the people of any country? It is clear, that as soon as the religious sentiment is awakened it needs guidance and enlightenment, that is, it needs a revelation; and no other revelation has been given but that through Jesus Christ. This sentiment, therefore, just as the sense of duty does, leads to faith in Him. If it does not lead to Him, then there is an instinct without an object, or without the means of attaining to its object.

But not only did we find the Baptist setting before his hearers what they ought to do, but also calling them to repentance. That is to say, as I have been putting it throughout this discourse, not only endeavoring to awaken within them the sense of duty, but also the sense of sin. The two are so closely connected that they may almost be regarded as two aspects of the same feeling. Regarding them however for this occasion separately, let us see how the latter also would lead to the object he had in view. A sense of our having done wrong, of our having wronged our Maker, wronged the nature He gave us akin to His own, fallen short of the opportunities He has presented to us, and wronged our fellow-men, can have but one issue, and that is the desire for atonement. If the uneasiness felt does not lead to this, it is purposeless. This seeking for atonement in a man who has become conscious of having done wrong is as natural as the effort to obtain food when one is hungry. All the penances and mortifications the natural man imposes on himself, all the altars that have been raised, and all the sacrifices that have been offered on every part of the earth's surface, are unanswerable witnesses to this fact. Man has felt universally the necessity of atonement. Man believes in God, and in a day of account. It cannot therefore be, he feels that it cannot be, a matter without issue that he has been a wrong-doer. How were the sins of that multitude that stood before John to be atoned for? He knew but of one way, the deliverance to be effected by Him to whom he pointed when he said, "Behold the Lamb of God which taketh away the sin of the world." And as there is no other name given under heaven whereby this may be effected, the sense of sin, accompanied, as it must be, by the craving for atonement and reconciliation, must lead to faith in Christ.

Every one, then, can and must judge for himself whether the ground I have been taking to-day is strong or weak. Each is, as far as he himself is concerned, the only possible judge of the matter. I appeal to what I suppose is in your hearts and minds, to what you must know about yourselves. But I have no fear that you will attempt to refute me from your own experience, for I have been speaking of the common principles and the common necessities of every man's nature. All languages show that men have in all times, and in all places, had an instinctive sense of duty. It matters nothing whether it results from the exercise of a congenital faculty, or from necessary development, as the flower and the fruit do from the seed. Certain actions and certain dispositions, varying from the necessity of circumstances within certain limits, but still always, however, varying, presenting the same characteristics, have always been approved of, well spoken of and regarded as becoming. To these men have considered themselves as under obligation. The sense, too, of man's standing in certain relations to God has been equally universal. The same is true of the sense of sin. Men are every where acquainted with its demerits, and have a more or less definite desire to be rid of what they anticipate as its consequences. Upon these principles of our common nature I take my stand. If you are conscious within yourselves of these feelings, there is but one legitimate conclusion to which you can come, that is, thankful and trustful faith in the Gospel of our Lord and Saviour Jesus Christ. It alone can give light accompanied with authority where we need them. It alone can supply those wants which conscience forces on our attention. Not only then is it the unspeakable gift of God, and emphatically the good tidings, but it is the necessary complement of our nature and of the conditions of our earthly existence. It is no by-thought or after-thought breaking in unexpectedly in the middle course of this present dispensation, but it is the completion and the crowning fact of the one great harmonious plan. Without it the moral and spiritual creation would be confusion, darkness, and despair. With it we obtain all that our spiritual and moral, and much that our intellectual nature requires—a sense of certainty, a sense of peace and reconciliation, and a sense that we are progressing towards a higher, and as we are allowed to hope, even a perfect state.

Observations on the foregoing Sermon.

We insist frequently upon the statement that the virtues are all of them fruits of faith. It therefore becomes necessary for the Minister who is desirous of fully instructing his hearers in the Word, to call their attention to the opposite view of the relation in which the two may be standing to each other; the relation in which that which is usually regarded as the cause appears as the effect, and the effect as the cause. And this will have the advantage of showing a scriptural, and I believe the readiest and most certain, because the natural method of producing faith in men's minds. To point out this method, and, while pointing it out, to use it for its proper purpose, as far as that can be done, is the object of the sermon.

It is surprising that the ideas of so many Christians as to what the religion of Christ requires of them should be so different from what we find Christ Himself telling us in His announcements of His kingdom and Gospel. He makes it consist in right conduct resulting from right dispositions. But if we listen now to those who put themselves most prominently before us as teachers of religion, and religious guides, we shall hear most of them affirming above all things the necessity of some detached doctrine, or the perversion of some doctrine, or some only partially true opinion. Such a text then as the one that has been before us is useful as bringing us back to a scriptural, and a plain and intelligible conception of Christianity. Here is the forerunner of Christ, whose work it was to prepare men for Christ, telling them what they must do; and what he tells them is that they must practise the several duties of their respective stations and circumstances.

There are some who in reading this sermon would remark that it is unmanly, and that it shows a distrust in the power of Christ, not to speak at once and in the first instance of Christ. It may not be so. He who on finding the surface of the ground unfit for supporting the structure he is desirous of erecting, goes down deeper for a foundation, is not to be accounted an unwise builder. At all events, such objectors are at issue with the Baptist in his method of bringing men to Christ.

I have just used, not undesignedly, the expression of going deeper for a foundation, because in these matters there is something anterior to, and more ancient than the Gospel, which is not yet two thousand years old; something more universal, for the Gospel has not yet spread over the world; something, in short, upon which the Gospel is founded, and to which it appeals—the sense of sin and the sense of duty, and the sense of our standing in certain relations to God. We may also regard these sentiments as the citadel. If the citadel be secured, the city may be lost, and again recovered. But if the citadel itself be lost, nothing more can be done. That which it was designed to protect has fallen with it, and all is lost.

STUDIES FOR SERMONS.

I WILL now give six short studies for sermons. I take them from a selection of as many hundreds. To make them intelligible to others, I am obliged to expand them very much beyond the length at which they were set down originally, when intended only for my own eye. I find studies of this kind of great use, because they enable one to take in at a glance all the ground that is to be passed over in preaching, and to judge in a few seconds of the quality and arrangement of one's materials.

It would be of advantage to very many also of those who read written discourses, if they were to make short abstracts of this kind of every sermon they write. It would oblige them to ascertain what is the real meaning of every paragraph; and to see what is the nature of its connection with what precedes and with what follows it. It would help them very much in forming a correct judgment; at all events it would necessitate their forming some kind of judgment of the sermon they were about to preach, both as a whole, and of each part of it.

STUDY I.

GOD HAS IMPORTANT WORK FOR THE LEAST AMONG US.

DEUTERONOMY vii. 6, 7.

"The Lord thy God hath chosen thee to be a special people unto Himself, above all people that are upon the face of the earth. The Lord did not set His love upon you, nor choose you, because ye were more in number than any people; for ye were the fewest of all people."

I.—1. THE gifts God bestows upon us, and the work He calls us to do, are not in proportion to our seeming importance in the world. Consider the history before us. He passes over the Egyptians, and chooses their wretched bondmen.

2. This may be further illustrated by the call of Abraham.

3. This is in accordance with what God does in the kingdoms of nature. The huge elephant is of very little use in the world, while the smallest animalcules have built up large districts of existing continents, and are building up what will be large districts of

future ones. The little bee gives men honey and light. Another insignificant insect contributes largely to the clothing of the human race. And so it is in the vegetable kingdom. The humble grass we tread on unnoticed has a more important place in the economy of nature than the stateliest trees of the forest.

II.—1. Just so, God has great work for little people to do. Consider what the world owes to the people described in the text as "the fewest of all people." Without them what would the religion of the leading races of mankind now be?

(2. It is instructive to observe, by the way, that though they did not comprehend their high calling, still God's purpose was worked out through them.)

III.—1. The moral of these observations is for each of us, that he cannot be so small but that God has some great work for him to do.

2. The humblest in circumstances should recollect, that it was not by the great, the powerful, the noble, that the Gospel was first received and exhibited to the world. The same glorious part is open to the humblest in all ages. It is so at this day.

3. God has something for the poor beggar to do, as a poor beggar, which he could not do were he a prince.

4. He who came in the form of a servant, not having where to lay His head, has shown by His

example, that a holy spirit will under the lowliest circumstances make its possessor a blessing to his fellow-men, and enable him to live to the glory of God.

IV. Nothing can so lift us above worldly cares and circumstances as the knowledge that, whatever our position at present, still that we have a part to act in the great plan, not unimportant, for assigned us by God Himself. We, even if we be the lowliest of all may do the work and live the life of God as thoroughly, may be as much His instruments, and represent Him as truly to our brethren, as the most exalted of all.

STUDY II.

SOME LIMITATIONS TO SELF-WILL.

DEUTERONOMY xii. 8.

"Ye shall not do after all the things that we do here this day, every man whatsoever is right in his own eyes."

I.—SELF-WILL is a natural impulse in all. It is not desirable, nor would it be possible that it should be carried out.

II.—1. Moses, in giving the Law which was to transform a multitude into a nation, announces the limitation it would set to their self-will. Without this limitation national existence would be impossible.

2. Look at the summary of the Law, the Decalogue, and see how its injunctions and prohibitions check and guide us at every step.

3. This is why we are told in the New Testament to be subject to magistrates; and that they are ordained of God.

4. The whole framework of human societies consists of so many checks on self-will. The same may

be said of our daily and hourly intercourse with each other.

5. Take what we are most familiar with, our own homes, and you will see that home becomes impossible if self-will is to be the rule of its member's conduct.

III.—But law is very imperfect. Religion, which substitutes the love of others for the love of self, is the only complete and ever-acting check. It transforms our worst fault into our highest grace.

IV.—The means by which we may be brought to this new birth, this regenerate state, are—(1) a knowledge of God; (2) thoughtful and serious habits of mind; (3) experience of the fact that self-will is not conducive to happiness; (4) early training; (5) an acquaintance with the character and with the work of Christ; (6) communion with God, i. e., prayer.

V.—The result will be, that a spirit—the opposite of self-will, originally external to ourselves, and no part of what we were by nature—God's Spirit will come and dwell with us, and make us one with God and one with Christ.

STUDY III.

WE TEMPT GOD BY OUR DESIRES.

PSALM cvi. 14, 15.

"They tempted God in the desert. And He gave them their desire; and sent leanness withal into their souls."

I.—1. THEN our having obtained our desires is no proof either that it was right to have entertained such desires, or that now they are fulfilled there will result to us from them any kind of blessing.

2. The text is a comment on the history recorded in the eleventh chapter of Numbers. While God, we are told, was bringing up the Israelites from the bondage of Egypt to the land He had promised them, He fed them in the desert with manna from heaven. This was to teach them their dependence on Him, and that they might trust Him. They desire meat instead. This, under ordinary circumstances, would have been a matter of indifference. Under the particular circumstances of the case it was tempting God. It was

calling upon Him to do in one way what He had for sufficient reasons decided would best be done in a different way. Their desire, however, is complied with; but its fulfilment is made the instrument of their punishment.

II.—1. It is then a sin to tempt God; and we tempt Him when we would do in one way what He has ordained should be done in another way. Jesus Christ would have tempted God if He had thrown Himself down from the pinnacle of the Temple, because reason (which God has given us for this among other purposes) teaches that those who act in this way, God does not protect.

2. God has ordained that man shall eat bread by the sweat of his brow. Those who make haste to get rich, and there are many such in these days, tempt God.

3. God has ordained that parents should train up their children by encouraging them in doing right, and by restraining them when they do wrong. Those who neglect these things tempt God.

4. God has ordained that we should hear the Lord Jesus Christ. Those who in this matter are in their own conceit wiser than God, are tempting God.

III.—1. But the text speaks of our desires as the means wherewith we may tempt God. Our desires may be in themselves all that is most excellent, as was the desire of Judas to be the companion of Jesus,

But desires the most excellent may, as in his case, be cherished for purposes the most vile.

2. Or our desires may be in themselves most wicked; as when the Israelites wished to worship idols or to be told smooth false things. So it may be with us when we desire opportunities for lust, revenge, deceit, &c.

3. Or they may be indifferent, as when we desire wealth; which may be desired and used either for good and godly purposes, or for bad and godless ones.

IV.—God, by the reason, the conscience, the powers of observation, the experience of life He has given us, and by the instruction and the Spirit He conveys to us through His Word, enables us to regulate our desires wisely. But at the same time, if we will have it so, He allows us opportunities for doing wrong, for wreaking our vengeance, for living unchastely, for deceiving, for self-indulgence, and for godlessness. How appalling is this thought! Let each then consider what is the nature of his desires, and why he wishes for such or such things. Let us look into our hearts. Self-knowledge is the most difficult, as it is the most useful of all knowledge. We must try to see ourselves as others see us, or rather as God sees us.

STUDY IV.

WHAT IS TRUTH?

JOHN xviii. 38.

"What is truth?"

I.—1. PILATE asked this question jeeringly, and did not wait for an answer. He was an educated Roman, and a man of the world. He must have had some acquaintance with the different schools of Greek philosophy. Probably he ridiculed them all for their disagreement as to what was the truth; and because each propounded as a rule of life what had no authority beyond that which resulted from its being the guess of the philosopher who had founded the school.

2. Pilate would perhaps have been a happier and a better man had he possessed the spirit of any one of the philosophers whose efforts to attain the truth he derided. But under the circumstances he was not to be blamed. And that he, an educated Roman, high in the service of the State, was not to be blamed for

speaking derisively of the truth, shows the necessity there was for the religion Christ came to establish.

II.—1. If Pilate could revisit this earth, how surprised would he be at the changes which have taken place in the world since he spoke the words before us! But perhaps neither the desolation of Judæa, nor the disappearance of the world-wide empire among the administrators of which he had held so high a place, would surprise him so much as that the Galilean peasant whose words he had derided had established a moral and spiritual empire in the world far wider than that of Imperial Rome, and was worshipped as God.

2. And how had this been effected? By the very truth he thought it so ridiculous that the Galilean peasant should make any pretensions of possessing.

III.—1. And in attaining to this dominion that truth was unaided by any kind of worldly power or inducement. The influence and authority of Government were opposed to it. The sword was drawn, not for it, but against it. And it had, besides, to combat both the wisdom and the vices of mankind. It triumphed entirely by its own intrinsic power, because it was the truth. It commended itself to the hearts and to the understandings of all men, because it was the truth.

2. Nations and races of men very unlike in many things have alike received this truth.

3. Nor have any diversities of condition or circumstances hindered men from embracing it.

IV.—1. And what is the substance of this truth? It consists, in its simplest expression, of two propositions. The first is what mankind had every where dimly apprehended,—that man is a sinner in the sight of God; and the second is what mankind had every where been seeking for,—that a way for reconciliation with God is now opened.

2. Texts on the latter point, 1 Timothy i. 15. John iii. 15. Matthew xi. 28.

3. This is what every thoughtful soul would regard as the gladdest of tidings, and what every dying soul sees is the main substance of the truth.

4. No philosophy can teach us any thing higher, and yet the most unlearned man can distinctly apprehend it.

V.—This truth has power to raise the beggar from the dunghill and to give him a place among princes, and to which many princes shall not attain. It makes those who receive it like Christ, and qualifies them for sitting with Him in heavenly places. It gives a man dominion over himself. It gives him the happiness of the world that now is, and of that which is to come. It harmonizes things temporal with things eternal. It reconciles man to God, and God to man.

STUDY V.

THE OFFENDER IN ONE POINT.

JAMES ii. 10.

"Whosoever shall keep the whole law, and yet offend in one point, is guilty of all."

I.—1. THE seeming hardness of this saying arises in a great measure from our translation. The word "point" suggests to us some small matter, but this word is not in the original. The literal translation would be "offend in one law;" i. e., the man who should keep nine of the commandments but break the tenth. This is a very different statement.

2. "Guilty of all" means that he has defied the authority upon which all the ten equally rest. So if he were tempted to break any other one, he would not be held back from doing it by the consideration that he would be breaking God's law.

II.—Another reason why we are offended at it is, that, as no one is without sin, in admitting it we condemn ourselves.

III.—1. We must endeavor to bring ourselves to acknowledge its force. Consider some of the figures used to express the relation in which we stand to God. We are called "the children of God." Can that child be regarded as affectionate, obedient, or dutiful towards his earthly father, who sets some one of his commandments at defiance?

2. We are "the servants of God." Suppose we had contracted to serve an earthly master, should not we break the contract and forfeit the stipulated compensation if we declined to do the whole of the work required of us?

3. We are "subjects of God's kingdom upon earth." It is no defence for the subject of an earthly kingdom, when charged with breaking any one of its laws, to allege that he has kept any number of its other laws. The forger cannot defend himself by saying, I am not a murderer or an adulterer.

4. This is the principle in accordance with which we judge others. We must so judge ourselves in respect of God's law.

IV.—1. This principle is not now announced here by St. James for the first time. It is as old as the Law itself, as quoted by St. Paul, "Cursed is every one that continueth not in all things which are written in the book of the law to do them."[1]

[1] Gal. iii. 10.

2. The Great Master also tells us, "Whosoever shall break one of these least commandments, and shall teach men so, he shall be called least in the kingdom of heaven."[2]

V.—1. The Herod who committed incest and beheaded John the Baptist is an instance of the insufficiency even of going so far as to hear gladly the most stirring preaching of the Word, and of doing much in conformity to it.

2. Judas supplies a case still more in point. It was the breach of the tenth commandment which literally made him guilty of others in so aggravated a form, that we see there was nothing to hold him back from the breach of any one, or of every one of them.

VI.—1. Another way of putting it. What is meant is the persistent breach of some commandment, any kind of sin practised habitually.

2. It is not said of those who, as Peter did, under some extraordinary circumstances bend before the storm; they soon recover their erect position.

3. Nor of those who have truly repented them of their former sins. It is the glad tidings of the Gospel, that they are freed from them, and are no longer under condemnation.

VII.—We must endeavor to picture to ourselves

[2] Matt. v. 19.

the mind, the character, the work of Christ. We must endeavor in every way we can to acquaint ourselves with God. So may we hope to be redeemed from every thing that is degrading, that is hateful, that is sinful.

STUDY VI.

GOD IS REVEALED TO US BY OUR HEARTS.

1 JOHN iv. 8.

"He that loveth not, knoweth not God."

I.—THE highest place is assigned in Holy Scripture to love, as a principle of conduct. It is the fulfilment of the whole Law. This seems to embrace every thing.

II.—1. This statement, however, of the Apostle John exalts love still higher. Love it is, he says, that reveals to us God.

2. This is the highest, and most precious, and most influential of all knowledge. No other knowledge so changes and so regenerates. Nothing so distinguishes man from the brute, or so lifts a man in thought and feeling above those in other respects his fellows.

III.—It is not, then, so much by reason that God is apprehended as by the heart. And this is a fact which our own experience confirms. Many a cultivated mind sees not, knows not God; but He is known by those who have loving hearts.

IV.—This justifies that dispensation of God which confines opportunities for mental culture to a few; for goodness of heart is placed within the reach of every one.

V.—1. It explains the coldness of the worldly and the recklessness of the sinner. Their hearts are hardened and corrupted, and so cannot reveal God to them.

2. The teaching, therefore, of the Ministers of the Word should not be denunciatory, but should aim at awakening a sense of gratitude and love.

3. There is much in every heart to which such teaching can appeal. In no one, probably, does God allow this witness to Himself to be completely silenced. He created the heart with a yearning for something to lean against, something to love. In the relations of home and of society, and even in the creatures and objects with which He surrounds us, He is ever endeavoring to call into exercise our good and loving feelings. But in connection with all these objects of love there arises a sense of imperfection and of perishableness, of insecurity and of uncertainty. No earthly friend can be worthy of the entire devotion of the heart. Nothing earthly can be secured to us but from day to day. Are we then to love those whom God has made near and dear to us less than we do at present? Nay,

with these words of the Apostle before us, we will strive to love them more ; knowing that this will ever be more and more distinctly revealing to us God, the one perfect and abiding object of love. "God is love;" and "he that loveth not, knoweth not God."

THE END.

READY IN OCTOBER (Continued).

LANGUAGE AND THE STUDY OF LANGUAGE. By WILLIAM DWIGHT WHITNEY, Professor of Sanscrit and Instructor in Modern Languages in Yale College. One volume, crown 8vo. Price, . $2 50.

Prof. Whitney's aim in these lectures is to place in a clearly comprehensible form, before the English reader and student, all the principal facts regarding language—its nature and origin, its growth, its classifications, its ethnological bearing, its value to man. Technical and metaphysical phraseology is avoided as much as possible and the progress of the argument is always from that which is well known, or obvious, to that which is more obscure or difficult. It is believed that the work will be widely adopted as a text-book for instruction.

FROUDE (J. A.) SHORT STUDIES ON GREAT SUBJECTS. One vol. crown 8vo. (Uniform with the History of England.) Price, $3.

The essays collected in this volume comprise all Mr. Froude's contributions to current periodical literature during the last few years. They are marked by that great originality and independence of thought, joined with stirring eloquence of expression which have secured him such wide and enduring reputation as an historian.

OLD ROMAN WORLD (The). The Grandeur and Failure of its Civilization. By JOHN LORD, LL.D. One vol. crown 8vo. Price, $3 00.

In this work Dr. Lord describes, in his peculiarly graphic and nervous style, "the greatness and misery of the old Roman world." The volume will be found entertaining instrrctive and profitable in the highest degree, while it will be specially useful as a text-book for higher schools and colleges.

PAULDING'S WORKS. TALES OF THE GOOD WOMAN. One vol. crown 8vo. (Uniform edition.) Price, . . $2 50.

IN NOVEMBER.

HISTORY OF THE CHURCH OF GOD during the period of Revelation. By CHARLES COLCOCK JONES, D. D. First Period. One volume, 8vo. Price, ... $3 50.

IK MARVEL. MY FARM AT EDGEWOOD. With 10 Photographic Illustrations by Rockwood, and a fine Portrait. In one vol. 4to. $10.

EXTEMPORARY PREACHING. By F. BARHAM ZINCKE, Vicar of Wherstead, and Chaplain in Ordinary to the Queen. (*Published by arrangement with the author.*) To be uniform with Bautain's Art of Extemporary Speaking. One vol. 12mo. Price, ... $1 75.

LANGE'S COMMENTARY. "GENESIS." "CORINTHIANS." Each one volume, royal 8vo. Price, per volume, ... $5 00.

THANKSGIVING: Memories of the Day, and Helps to the Habit. By WILLIAM ADAMS, D. D. One volume, 12mo. Price, $2 00.

IN DECEMBER.

LANGE'S COMMENTARY. "THESSALONIANS." "TIMOTHY." "TITUS." "HEBREWS." One volume, royal 8vo. Price, . $5 00.

PAULDING'S (J. K.) WORKS. DUTCHMAN'S FIRESIDE. One vol. crown 8vo. Price, ... $2 50.

www.ingramcontent.com/pod-product-compliance
Lightning Source LLC
LaVergne TN
LVHW010221110826
845151LV00004B/1171
* 9 7 8 1 4 2 5 5 2 7 1 7 4 *